Breaking
the Death Habit

Breaking the Death Habit

The Science of Everlasting Life

LEONARD ORR

edited by
Kathy Glass

Frog, Ltd.
Berkeley, California

Breaking the Death Habit
The Science of Everlasting Life

Published by Frog, Ltd.

Frog, Ltd. books are distributed by
North Atlantic Books
P.O. Box 12327
Berkeley, CA 94712

Cover art by Spain Rodriguez
Cover and book design by Paula Morrison

Printed in the United States of America

Library of Congress Cataloging-in-Publication Data
Orr, Leonard
    Breaking the death habit : the science of everlasting life
    / Leonard Orr.
        p. cm.
    ISBN 1-883319-68-4
    1. Immortalism.   2. Spiritual life.   I. Title.
BF1999.066   1998
291.2'3—dc2   97-39685
                                                     CIP

1 2 3 4 5 6 7 8 9 / 02 01 00 99 98

Table of Contents

Author's Foreword ... vii

Preface by Bob Frissell ... xi

Part I—About Physical Immortality

Introduction ... 3

1. The Components of Physical Immortality ... 7

2. Immortal Yogis: The Living Masters ... 15

3. Beyond Senility and Aging ... 21

4. Spiritual Purification: The Essentials ... 27

5. The Failure of Religion ... 39

6. The Death of Jesus Christ ... 43

Part II—Great Immortals of the East: A Sampler

7. Babaji ... 49

8. Bhartriji ... 63

9. Goraknath ... 71

10. Immortality: The Stages of Mastery ... 77

Part III—Suggested Practices for Spiritual Purification

11. Spiritual Breathing ... 85

12. Fire ... 93

13. The Name of God ... 99

14. Further Suggestions for Spiritual Purification ... 103

15. Personal Mastery and Citizenship ... 121

16. Conclusion: So You're Immortal—What's Next? ... 129

Author's Foreword

THIS BOOK IS a practical discussion of the basic ideas and practices for personal mastery and health. I have presented here the minimum foundation for personal immortality, which I learned from true immortal yogis. These practices are also referred to if not explicitly described in the Bible and all great scriptures. For example, Elijah was the fire master of the Bible, but nowhere does he discuss the theory of fire purification or the spiritual power of fire.

I believe we are moving into a new age of physical immortality and personal mastery—an age of divine human beings who don't forget their humanity. God has been systematically working behind the scenes of human history. He/she is the God of science and technology and even the United Nations as well as religion, or he/she is no God at all. The governments of the world do God's will for the enlightenment of individuals. It has to be a gradual process. It is invisible except to those who have eyes to see.

God has given us the practical tools to be immortal. The bottleneck is dead orthodoxies, philosophies, and beliefs, not only in churches, but in education, science, business, and government.

After meeting and studying eight immortal yogis who mastered over 300 years in the same body, I condensed the common denominators that make them immortal. I present those principles to you here. They are simple and pleasurable to work with. If the path of physical immortality were not pleasurable then the Creator would be a sadist who requires eternal pain and misery. The spiritual practices that make us immortal are so simple, they are easy to ignore. This is how physical death became so popular.

Being immortal is on the same level of difficulty as earning a living or supporting a family. It takes focus and self-discipline, along with a certain amount of intelligence and endurance, to raise children and pay their bills through college. Becoming an immortal yogi master may be easier than this, but it takes focus and persistence in the right habits. I call them the habits of personal aliveness and the disciplines of pleasure. You will learn what they are in this book.

My central point is that victory over death is within your reach. I describe the spiritual purification practices used by all the immortal yogis I have met in terms of Western civilization. Our civilization can either suck away our life energy and kill us, or support our everlasting life in comfort and pleasure. It is up to you! You can focus on life and mastery or defeat and death. Obviously, the more people who adopt this focus on personal immortality and mastery, the easier it becomes for all of us. Although some of the immortal yogis participate for many years in society, it is definitely easier for them to live in small, supportive communities in the Himalaya, for example.

To get everyone in a small town or large city engaged in a dialogue about physical immortality and personal mastery is an intelligent contribution to your own survival. But it is not necessary or perhaps even feasible to persuade anyone to be immortal. Some people desire to die and they deserve this right. However, everyone deserves the right to choose life or death. Without the information in this book, people do not have a meaningful choice.

Most people are too immersed in the death urge and death consciousness to care about immortal yogis or even their own divine potential. Unfortunately, mass death urge has a tendency to precipitate disasters. The best thing you can do for the health of a neighborhood or a nation is to master and spread the ideas of physical immortality and voluntary spiritual purification before God makes it involuntary. Physical death in all its forms is involuntary purification.

May the new millennium bring us all mastery and longevity!

Preface

1. First Meeting

IN 1979 LEONARD ORR came into my life, and I have never been the same. Leonard is a mind-blower. He has the ability to alter reality. If you enter into a relation with him with any degree of sincerity, you will be mutated. Stuff is going to come up in his presence—anything that is less pure than he is—and you are going to have to address it.

Reading this book is entering into a relationship with him.

On the fateful evening of our initial meeting I went with two friends to something called a "money seminar" at Leonard's legendary rebirthing center, the Theta House in San Francisco. At an old Victorian at 301 Lyon Street across from the Panhandle leading into Golden Gate Park, we found our way up to a large attic. Leonard was quite a draw in the late '70s; it was standing room only, at least eighty people.

Each visitor was handed Leonard's strange pamphlet, "The Prosperity Consciousness Consultation." The seminar consisted of this essay being read aloud by various participants. Discussion of ideas and questions followed.

For the most part, Leonard just sat in the front of the room exuding a Cheshire smile. Near the end, to my astonishment, he gave everyone an opportunity to pay him again, anything from a dollar to a hundred dollars. Considering that those in attendance had already shed a fifteen-dollar entry fee for the attic, it seemed crazy that anyone would choose to lay down more. It stunned me to watch people literally lining up for the privilege of paying Leonard money.

Meanwhile Leonard was sporting a newly shaved head; he was also wearing a green sweater with dollar signs all over it (no kidding). I later discovered that the shaving was a spiritual purification technique passed directly to him by Babaji—but it must be done consciously. Your crown chakra is constantly being impressed by programs that are encoded in your hair. When you shave your head, it stops receiving those old impressions.

Leonard just sat there and smiled, accepting each dividend in turn.

The second time I went to hear Leonard I came prepared to "donate." I didn't know why—perhaps just to see what it felt like. So, I had twenty-five dollars on me, fifteen to get in the door plus an additional ten for Leonard. I brought my long-time friend Ila. Just before we got to the discussion, I asked Ila if she could lend me ten dollars. I suddenly had an irrational desire to give Leonard twenty dollars instead of ten. My companion must have thought I was crazy, but she reluctantly dug a ten out of her purse.

At the appropriate moment I got in line with my two tens. In 1979, that was a lot of cash for me—thirty-five bills when you count the fifteen to get in the door. Long ago I had learned that a footloose life was more meaningful to me than accumulating equity, especially if the latter meant doing something unpleasant or tedious. A day in an ancient redwood grove or by the great Pacific was more lucrative (spiritually anyway) than working. As Leonard would later note, I was in transition from conditioned motivation—an automaton following instructions and reinforced by money—to divine motivation, whereby work is an expression of my authority and true nature.

Leonard was wearing his green $ sweater again, his head

freshly reshaved. As I stood in line I sensed doubts creeping in: "This is loco. What am I doing?"

Then it came my turn to pay. I felt embarrassed, stupid, intimidated, weird, frightened, you name it! I could barely look at Leonard; yet I was somehow able to hand him twenty dollars. He just sat there and smiled.

Leonard has the capacity to shatter your view of reality in a multitude of ways. I later learned that he is an expert in group synergy. As he would explain it, whenever two or more people gather, there is an exchange of energy. If the other person is more conscious than you are, what you will feel is your own aroused energy, i.e., your fears and limitations. When you get to the point where you can just "be" with that person, you have moved through or integrated the particular set of fears associated with his or her presence. The money ritual was part of this process, a ceremony by which Leonard shepherded my introduction into what you might call "guru consciousness."

2. Rebirthing

The mind and the breath are the King and Queen of human consciousness.—Leonard Orr

When I met Leonard that evening at the Panhandle, I went solely to hear about money. Yet he began the evening talking about breathing. "Breathing," I wondered, "what's that got to do with anything? I came here to get my money case handled—let's get on with it!" Later I would discover that the answer to my question was "Everything!" But at the time I had no idea—I thought I knew how to breathe, and I figured everyone else did too.

Later that evening Leonard announced that he would be conducting a year-long program beginning in March 1980. The purpose of this program was to train rebirthers and seminar leaders. For only one thousand dollars a month we would have the privilege of learning directly from him.

I could barely give him twenty dollars—how could I ever give him one thousand dollars? Of course, I ended up joining the program.

Rebirthing, as it turns out, is the single most important thing I have ever learned. It is an ancient technique—at least so my intuition tells me. In a book entitled *Rebirthing According to Spirit*, the channeled entity Mother Mary relates how rebirthing "was practiced by the Essenes ... many thousands of years ago, even before the Master Jesus came onto this planet." Another of the channeled entities, Cochise, adds, "There is one who is known as Thoth, who is the vibration of the Atlantean, who is one of the master spirits that brought the whole process of rebirthing into knowingness, or into material form."

Leonard Orr, however, is the modern-day founder of rebirthing. He fills that role for two basic reasons: first, because he had one of the most difficult births imaginable, and second, because he learned to view that experience not from the standpoint of victimization but as an opportunity to change the basic conditions of his life.

According to Leonard:

> My mother had her first three children—girls—almost exactly eighteen months apart. Then she decided she had enough children. In spite of this decision she had three more.... I was the last. An unwanted child after my mother had held the decision to have no more children for twelve years.
>
> Through rebirthing I have remembered a lot. I have remembered coming into her womb and feeling excited about being back in the physical universe. But my joy soon turned into trouble when I discovered I was an unwelcome guest. When my mother found out I was

there during the second or third month of pregnancy, she was very upset. This is when my miseries began in this life. Later, I concluded that the only way I could please my mother was to disappear—to kill myself. I tried to hang myself on my umbilical cord. It was an unsuccessful attempt. I was a breach birth with the cord wrapped around my neck three times. At birth I came as close to dying as is possible without actually dying. The cord was around my neck so tight that the doctor decided to pull me out by my legs far enough to cut the umbilical cord. He then pushed me back in, turned me around and pulled me out with forceps. I have relived much of my womb life, birth and infancy during my rebirthing healing process. I never felt welcome in my family and most of the time I still don't....

My birth was a long one. I remember the suffocation. I remember my mother's shame at having her legs spread. At one point in 1977 I had a rash around my neck in three stripes, which was a physiological memory of the umbilical cord.

Leonard Orr developed rebirthing over a thirteen-year period as a result of his experiences of his own birth memories. His flashbacks began in 1962, when he suddenly couldn't get out of his bathtub. He says he stayed there for two hours before he had enough strength to climb free.

Between 1962 and 1975 Leonard had numerous other re-birthing experiences. One of the most dramatic occurred in 1973 when, as the result of a terrible headache, he intuitively decided to get down on his hands and knees with his head hung down so it touched the floor. As a birth memory seared through him, the pain immediately stopped. In Leonard's own words:

In 1974 I gave a spiritual psychology seminar. I talked about my birth memories and most of the people attending wanted to have birth memories too. I told them to get into their bathtubs and sit there until they felt it was time to get out. Then, to stay in the tub thirty minutes to an hour longer. The feeling that we must get out is an urgency barrier. Every time we sit through an urgency barrier we get a fantastic realization about ourselves and we learn about another program that is controlling us. This was the first technique of Rebirthing: to just sit and meditate in the bathtub through an urgency barrier.

Most of the people in the seminar group tried this experiment and had such powerful emotional releases that they wished someone had been there to talk with them about what was happening to them. I volunteered. I experimented with Rebirthing people this way. It was very powerful.

Later I got the idea of using a snorkel and nose clips in a hot tub. When I put people into the water, they were in a womb-like environment and they instantly regressed to birth and prenatal states of consciousness. They did not just have memories, they regressed to a psycho-physical state. It was a complete spiritual, mental and physical experience. People had a completed energy cycle which was an integrated healing experience. I stayed with each person until they felt peace. They experienced the peace that surpasses all understanding....

In 1975, after giving hundreds of hot tub Rebirths, I noticed people having a "healing of the breath" experience. I realized their breathing mechanism was totally transformed and their mind-body-spirit relationship was forever transformed. This healing took place after several sessions—when they felt safe enough to relive the moment of their first breath. Most people feel fear during this moment, so they have to feel safe to reach it.

They all breathed in a certain rhythm. It was a connected rhythm in which the inhale was merged with the exhale in one breath. It was the unity of Being experienced physiologically. It was the merging of the inner breath—life energy—with the outer breath—air and the breathing mechanism.

From the very beginning it was my goal to make people spiritually self-sufficient with Energy Breathing. That is, to give them enough sessions until they could Rebirth themselves.

Next I experimented with this connected breathing rhythm without the water and found that it was much better to do ten one- to two-hour Connected Breathing sessions out of the water before giving people a session in a hot tub with nose clips and a snorkel. Dry Rebirthing was born. This made it possible for Rebirthing to become a mass movement. Getting in a hot tub, nude except for a snorkel and nose clips, and reliving your birth, was a little esoteric for most people. But now all people had to do was lie down and breathe and they could have the most marvelous experience of their life.

Let's say you have a glass of water with a layer of mud on the bottom (old stuck energy) and you begin pouring in a constant stream of fresh water (new energy); the first thing that happens is the mud gets stirred up, clouding the water. As you continue pouring in the fresh water, eventually all the mud gets flushed out and you are left with a glass of fresh, pure water.

In rebirthing, *prana* or life-force energy is the equivalent of fresh water; old stuck energy from birth and parental conditioning is thick mud. When the strata of mud sticks at the bottom of the glass, your prana is suppressed. When the mud is being stirred around by the flow of fresh water, you enter a transitional state called activation. Once all the mud has been flushed out and you are left with a glass of pure, fresh water, and you cross over into a state of integration or completion.

What Leonard discovered through his bathtub experiments was that prior to proper breathing, one's stuck energy is physically held in place by shallow breathing; this is the mechanism of suppression. In such a state we are barely able to function.

Our lives are shaped by, formed by, and molded by stuck energy in ways that limit our expression and individuation. The stuck energy also bears tension and painful bodily symptoms, eventually leading to disease and ultimately degenerative illness and death.

In rebirthing, there is a freeing of the breath session by session. Most people can have a thorough experience of what it means to breathe prana as well as air in their first guided rebirthing session. A permanent transformation usually takes place sometime between the third and tenth session.

It should be noted that prana is even more vital for our existence than air. We cannot exist for even one second without it. While we do take in prana along with the air we breathe, we do it unconsciously, and we breathe it in infinitesimally small amounts—just enough to keep the body alive but not enough to even begin to experience its incredible healing capabilities.

Healing comes about as a direct result of breathing prana and of psychophysically reliving the moment of the first breath. In this crucible the breathing mechanism goes from exhale-oriented to inhale-oriented. In exhale-oriented breathing, you slowly push the exhale out, and after a long pause, inhale a small amount of air—almost as an afterthought. It is an act literally of holding your breath, but it is the only way to keep your birth trauma suppressed.

In addition, exhale-oriented breathing is death-oriented breath insofar as it fills the cells with an excess of carbon dioxide. It takes an average of seventy years to complete the job. The birth trauma by then has become a self-fulfilling prophecy. Inhale-oriented breathing emphasizes pulling on the inhale and relaxing on the exhale and keeping them the same length. Your breathing becomes efficient as you use all your energy for the inhale. Exerting effort on the exhale is unnecessary because gravity and your natural muscle contractions do it for you. All your life energy is conserved for the inhale, leading to a life-oriented breath.

Additionally, you are filling cells with oxygen, which they greatly prefer to carbon dioxide. Breathing efficiently you are dispersing prana, flushing the circulatory, nervous, and respiratory systems as well as the aura or energy body.

Proper breathing cleanses psychic dirt, negative mental mass, physical tension, physical illness, and emotional problems from human consciousness; yet most people go through a lifespan not knowing—and not knowing that they don't know—the healing power contained in the conscious use of their breath. This teaching is Leonard's greatest gift.

Leonard's foundation of rebirthing is a simple exercise of twenty connected breaths. You can do it throughout the day, whenever you feel the need. However, it is recommended that for the first week you do it only once daily:

1. Take four short breaths.
2. Then take one long breath.
3. Pull the breaths in and out through your nose.
4. Do four sets of the five breaths, that is, four sets of four short breaths followed by one long breath without stopping, for a total of twenty breaths.

Merge the inhale with the exhale so the breath is connected without any pauses. One inhale connected to one exhale equals one breath. All twenty breaths are connected in this manner so you have one series of twenty connected breaths with no pauses. Consciously pull the inhale in a relaxed manner and let go completely on the exhale, while continuing to keep the inhale and exhale the same length. Use the short breaths to emphasize the connecting and merging of the inhale and the exhale into unbroken circles. Use the long breath to fill your lungs as completely as you comfortably can on the inhale, and to let go completely on the exhale.

Breathe at a speed that feels natural for you. It is important that the breathing be free, natural, and rhythmical, rather than forced or controlled. This is what enables you to breathe prana as well as air. Since most of you have developed bad breathing habits, you might experience some physical sensations such as lightheadedness or tingling sensations in your hands or elsewhere. If you do this exercise daily, you will notice that the sensations may change and become less overwhelming, and more generative of healing. This indicates that you are learning about breathing consciously and are getting direct benefits in your body. Daily practice of this exercise will teach you more about breathing than you have ever learned in your entire life. If you wish to accelerate the process, contact a professional rebirther and schedule a series of one- to two-hour guided sessions.

Another breathing exercise, Alternate Nostril Breathing, came to me from Leonard, who received it from Goraknath:

Inhale through the left nostril and exhale through the right nostril. Then inhale through the right nostril and exhale through the left nostril. Repeat this cycle three or nine times. Make the breaths as long as you comfortably can. You can either hold the inhale, or you can connect the inhale to the exhale as in twenty connected breaths.

Goraknath said that this exercise, when practiced daily, along with chanting *Om Namaha Shivai,* is enough to keep a constant flow of life energy in the body and create immortality. This exercise cleans the *nadis,* a series of organs inside the nostrils which send life energy to all the organs of the body. Do this exercise three or nine times a day for three months in order to experience a cleaning of the internal organs of the nostrils (nadis). Then do it for as long as you want to keep your body.

When you begin Leonard's rebirthing breath cycle—that is, pulling on the inhale, relaxing on the exhale, and breathing in a connected or circular manner with no pause—the inhale merges into and becomes the exhale, and the exhale merges into and becomes the inhale. As you continue this, you begin to feel a tingling and vibrating sensation in various parts of or throughout your body. Also, a layer of the old stuck energy begins to get stirred up, arising from suppression into a state of activation. In medical terms, this is known as hyperventilation. It is defined as over-breathing and is considered to be a disease.

In *Breath Awareness* Leonard compiled a list of symptoms associated with the hyperventilation syndrome. They include:

Rapid breathing
Forced or heavy breathing
Involuntary breathing
Difficulty with breathing, including asthma attacks
Tingling or vibrating sensations in hands or feet
Choking
Tetany (a medical term for temporary paralysis or cramps)
Light-headedness or dizziness
Hysterical crying
Irrational feelings of fear or terror
Fainting
Out-of-body experiences
Temporary insanity
Localized feelings of extreme pressure on body parts
Strong energy flows
Fluctuating body temperature
Extreme sweating or inconsolable cold
Confusion
Claustrophobia
Headache
Body rushes
Full-body orgasmic feelings

Spiritual or religious visions
Dramatic telepathic experiences
Nausea
Dryness of mouth
Buzzing or ringing in the ears
Birth memories or dream-like states
Euphoria and blissful states
Color fantasies and vivid color perception
Muscle spasms including epileptic-type seizures
Death and resurrection experiences

Hyperventilation is not a disease. It is a healing in process to counteract the fact that you have subventilated all your life. It is also the healing in process for the damage done to your breathing mechanism during birth. One of the hyperventilation symptoms most people go through is a phenomenon called tetany—a temporary involuntary tightening or paralysis of the joints, usually in the hands and face. This is your body's way of showing you how much you have been "holding on" all your life. If you resist the paralysis, you can lock yourself up in tetany to the point where you feel as though you will never move again. The way out is always through rather than away from the feeling. If you can allow yourself to have a thorough experience of what you would normally tend to resist, the tetany will disappear.

Rebirthing is a two-stage process. The first is learning to breathe energy (life force energy, or prana) as well as air. The second is, in Leonard's words, "to unravel the birth-death cycle, and to incorporate the body and mind into the conscious life of the Eternal Spirit, to become a conscious expression of the Eternal Spirit."

Leonard continues:

"Rebirthing as unraveling the birth-death cycle takes longer than learning to breathe energy.... It involves personal liberation from birth trauma, infancy consciousness, family patterns, and the death urge. It involves mind and body mastery."

In order to understand what is meant by this, we need to dig deeper and get an understanding of these inhibiting factors that have literally kept us asleep and unconscious far too long.

3. Breaking the Death Habit

> *Physical immortality is the only cause you can't die for.*—Leonard Orr

There is yet another factor that keeps us from living out the experience of our full aliveness—the unconscious death urge. As Leonard used to say, "Unless your parents are immortal, you have inherited a death urge."

The death urge is a real psychic entity that literally can be isolated in your own mind and destroyed. Composed of anti-life thoughts and beliefs, it is held in place by the belief that death is inevitable and out of your control. Its purpose is to kill you, and that is exactly what it will do, unless you kill it first.

If your thoughts, feelings, and actions unerringly create your reality (and they do!), then the unquestioned, unexamined death urge that you inherited as a multi-generational pattern from your parents and from the culture will become an unwitting context for your life, and it will produce its intended result. The ultimate victim is someone who believes it is someone or something "out there" that has control over him or her.

Whether or not you gain immortality, there is tremendous power in simply questioning the inevitability of death. Consider that the source of victim consciousness might just be the belief that you have no say in the health, well-being, and destiny of your body.

If you want to take control of your life, you must open yourself to the possibility that it is you who creates your own safety and well-being—you and no one else. It is you who creates your own health and aliveness and illness, injury, accidents, as well as the death of your physical body.

Leonard was teaching people to defy their seemingly inevitable death sentence. That is, he was teaching how to break agreements we have unwittingly and unconsciously entered into by the very nature of being at the effect of the birth-death cycle. This is Leonard's genius. You may or may not believe in the radical act he is teaching, but if you entertain it, you will change in unimaginable ways.

There is no halfway position here. Either you are willing to break the death habit or you are not. I will adopt a position somewhat separate from Leonard and say: even if you do eventually die, you can still break the death habit first—i.e., death consciousness.

Breath, birth, money, and death are part of a single cycle.

Breaking the death habit also leads to dissolving the birth trauma and manifesting affluence. New Age televangelists talk these days about the spiritual sources of prosperity and wealth. Leonard came first; Leonard is the originator; Leonard is the Real McCoy. More than that, he is one of the inaugurators of the entire consciousness movement. Parroting and opining nothing, he as much as—if not more than—the late, highly publicized Timothy Leary and that new kid on the block, Deepak Chopra, understood the real karmic nuclear spiritual laws of money and success.

How can you be fully alive and aware and prosper if you haven't unraveled your death urge? If you are unaware of it, it is unconsciously producing results. Furthermore, the more enlightened you become, the more activated the death urge becomes. Anything you are still subconsciously holding onto that is less pure than your highest thoughts is fair game to come to your attention. And since you are becoming more conscious, your thoughts are becoming more powerful and they will manifest more quickly. So if you have never questioned death, you are unwittingly at its effect.

You will probably rationalize too and conclude that since you will be meeting your maker, it must be for the highest good. If you really want to meet your maker, go for full aliveness so you can ascend there!

Physical immortality is living as long as you want, and wanting to live as long as you do. It is leaving when you choose, and doing it consciously via resurrection or ascension. Physical immortality creates a conscious context for your life fully supportive of your aliveness—one that is broad enough even to include the death urge. That means when any life-negating thought comes to your attention, you will be able to include it in a setting of awareness, safety, and trust. That in turn will allow you to relax and breathe into it so you can experience it fully in the process of letting it go. In so doing, you can unravel your death urge one thought at a time.

Leonard said that rebirthing never could have happened had he not first unraveled his death urge, a process which climaxed for him in 1967. From the beginning, the idea of immortality has been contained in rebirthing. Immortality creates the certainty of safety by posing a context broad enough to include anything that might come up.

After liberating himself from his death urge, Leonard became fascinated with the idea of physical immortality. But one problem he encountered was that the authors of most of the books he read on the subject had died. One person, a Divine Science minister by the name of Harry Gaze, who had written a book called *How to Live Forever,* died on the way to the second in a series of lectures he was giving on the subject at the Hollywood Church of Religious Science.

Leonard declared he could not trust these people. He developed a new set of criteria. He decided not to believe anyone unless they were actually doing it. He arbitrarily picked three hundred years as the minimum qualifying age. This led him to the only place he knew where actual immortals hang out.

Leonard went to India in the spring of 1977 but didn't find any immortals. A female traveling companion did, however. She was guided by Babaji, who had materialized to her twice before the trip. After spending seven months with Babaji, she returned to California with pictures and reports. Her transformation included having been dematerialized by Babaji for a three-day tour of the universe!

As a result of this woman's shared experiences, Leonard immediately tuned into Babaji's energy and has kept a very powerful spiritual relationship with him ever since. Leonard was planning another trip to India in December of 1977, but because he was very busy, he considered cancelling. Then, when the time came to make his final decision, while he was meditating in a friend's house in Houston, Texas, Babaji appeared to him and stayed for three minutes. That experience changed his mind. Leonard said it made him realize how limited his thinking was.

He went to India subsequently and spent a month with Babaji. When Leonard was with this immortal he questioned him about rebirthing. He recounts this conversation:

> Before I met Babaji in the flesh, I had figured out that breathing in cooperation with the mind was the key to the health of the body and mind. I had concluded that the Breath of Life could be the "Fountain of Youth" and, therefore, the key to the eternal life of the body as well as the mind. Since Babaji has mastered the eternal life of the spirit, mind and body, his body, though thousands of years old, has the appearance and integrity of a young man.

So, one day in January 1978, I mustered enough courage to test my conclusions with Babaji. It took courage on my part, because if anyone on Earth could invalidate my cherished logic, it would be him. I had tested my ideas upon thousands of the world's greatest minds, but he was the first genuine immortal I had met.

I said: "Does rebirthing produce Mritenjaya?" [which means victory over death].

He said: "Rebirthing produces Mahamritenjaya." [which means supreme victory over death].

I said: "You mean, since prana is eternal, the body with prana is eternal?"

He said: "Of course." And walked away as if the conversation were mundane.

To me, the confirmation of my ideas from an actual immortal was a big deal. But to him, I concluded, it has been simple and obvious for thousands of years. To him, it was a stupid question.

Leonard realized that Babaji was the greatest thing on the planet, and he decided to go back and spend at least one month with him every year. Every time he went, he said, it was tempting just to stay there and forget about the rest of the world. He also said that Babaji has given him opportunities to ascend.

In the course of his yearly treks to India, Leonard has now met eight individuals who meet his minimum qualification of three hundred years in the same body. The youngest immortal master Leonard met was three hundred years old. He would not let visitors closer than fifty yards. When asked the secret of his longevity, his reply was, "Stay away from humans."

Another, Bhartriji, was given immortality by Babaji in 56 BC. At the time he was emperor of all of India, but according to Leonard, he renounced his kingdom and became a *saddhu*. A saddhu is a person who gives up his worldly possessions in order to practice spiritual purification full-time, while living off the land. Even though he has powers of ascension, Bhartriji has maintained a local address here on planet Earth for more than two thousand years. His ashram is located in a forest reserve of one hundred square miles. It has been reported that although the reserve contains wild animals, no human has ever been attacked by them. Bhartriji is quietly doing his job. He has a very soft, gentle, and innocent presence. Leonard said Bhartriji felt as though he had been working on himself for two thousand years, yet he has an ageless and tension-free body.

One of Babaji's many manifestations, according to Leonard, was Goraknath, who has trained numerous immortals. If you go to one of Goraknath's students for instruction, your first lesson will be to work continuously with the mantra Om Namaha Shivai. Then, if you are serious, you may come back in three years for your next lesson.

Thus the remembrance of God's name is the first of the common practices. Then comes the awareness of the energy body, for the energy body is the secret to the physical body. Becoming aware of the energy body is the key to reversing the aging process and mastering the health of the body. Next comes the realization that the conscious use of the elements earth, air, water, fire, and prana (or ether) can cleanse the energy body or aura more efficiently than the mind. They blow away, wash away, burn away, etc., all the negative energy concentrations, for they are the physical aspects of the One Spirit.

Much of what I have said in this preface to *Breaking the Death Habit* can be found in a somewhat different form within my published books. I thought long and hard about whether to say something totally new here, but I finally decided that I had paid my most sincere homage to Leonard in my existing writing. I did not want to appear in his book with anything less.

If it is not already clear to you, I owe Leonard everything. Of course, I also owe him nothing. We are all part of a long transmission of undoing the great forgetting and reclaiming our dignity and destiny. Leonard has been a master remember-berer, and he has enabled others to remember. I now remember, thanks to Leonard. I could not have written my books without his coming first and leading our revolt.

—Bob Frissell,
author of *Nothing in This Book Is True, But It's Exactly How Things Are* and *Something in This Book Is True....*

About Physical Immortality

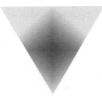

Introduction

Is PHYSICAL IMMORTALITY REALISTIC? The immortal yogis of this world and I are here to tell you it is. Of course, in this day and age, physical immortality is an idea you have to get used to. It is a problem that can keep you busy for a few million years.

It is time for this idea to once again become widespread. For much of recent human history, most people have been immersed in mortal, deathist mentality. Physical death as we know it today has been popular for only five thousand years. We don't know what will happen when physical immortality becomes popular again.

Our materialistic civilization has a tendency to solidify the death urge. But immortalists reject the idea that death is inevitable, saying instead that death is controlled by individual consciousness. Immortal mentality is made possible as a function of changing your thoughts, freeing your breath, and establishing an eternal self-image. The immortals know that death is only for people who persist in and love ignorance. Death is for people who love the superficial pleasures of the body more than the eternal pleasures of the spirit.

Conquering death is the basic intelligence test in the physical universe. Physical immortality is the first step in any practical spiritual enlightenment.

Most people die before they question the idea that death is inevitable, even though they think that they are spiritually enlightened. But the idea of physical immortality is not enough. Developing a philosophy of physical immortality is the first step. The second step is to unravel the personal death urge absorbed from family tradition—the psychology of physical immortality. The third step is to develop mastery of the physical body—the physiology of physical immortality. The third step is where practical spiritual purification exercises come in. For example, breath mastery teaches the cleansing of the mind and body in an easy, practical way. Fasting further cleans the blood. Mastery of sleep teaches, among other things, the mastery of the astral world, which most people think is the world of the dead. Water and fire purification are basic. More on this in upcoming pages.

My purpose is not to put down the practice of physical death. Physical death is a great invention that permits people to leave planet Earth who don't like being here. Most people seem to be more afraid of living with themselves forever than of physical death.

Note that you are presently immortal until you prove otherwise. Dying is more difficult than living. We begin with the following affirmation, which has saved thousands of people from death. I recommend that you memorize it and master it through meditation: *I am alive now. Therefore, my life urges must be stronger than my death urges. As long as I strengthen my life urges and weaken my death urges, I will go on living in increasing health and youthfulness.*

Adding the words "physical immortality" to everyone's vocabulary is a worthy educational goal. The realization that our own mind is the greatest threat to the health and aliveness of our physical body is a thought everyone deserves to have.

These simple concepts are our spiritual birthright. The reason more people in the Western world have not conquered death is simply because so few are working on it. Most people have surrendered to the idea that death is inevitable and beyond our control. This popular idea is taught by most religious organizations even though the Saviors or Saints of all great religions have conquered death. The idea is also taught in the public schools. We program our children for death. When we trade in our unconscious death urge for physical immortality philosophy and spiritual purification practices, we can achieve personal aliveness, youthfulness, and body mastery more consciously.

War is a social expression of personal death urge. But we have the opportunity to achieve world peace now. This information about physical immortality is desperately needed to realize peace in all countries.

We have so many modern life-support systems built into our civilization that the majority of people may be able to realize physical immortality today as they did in the days of Ram and Sita, when everyone knew that physical death was optional. A person with indoor plumbing, hot water, and a fireplace has the most sophisticated "immortal yogi cave" ever developed. Our religion and philosophy just need to catch up with scientific progress. The tragedy of our generation is that people are dying needlessly in ignorance just because they have never heard nor thought about the idea of physical immortality. We could have heaven on Earth if people were as committed to health and love and aliveness as they are to ignorance, negative thoughts, and dying and going to heaven.

Don't forget that physical immortality is not the ultimate goal. It is a natural benefit of being a good person and following the rules of healthy living. Living longer is not the goal of physical immortality. Increasing the quality of one's life is the goal—the present-time quality of personal existence in spirit, mind, and body. Physical immortality releases us from the prison of living under the sentence of death. Most people are living on "death row" and wonder why their life doesn't work. Finding eternal life in the human heart is the source of health in the mind and body.

As the Bible says over and over, "The gift of Eternal Life may be yours." (See, for example, John 3:16.) Eternal Life means to incorporate the body into the conscious life of the Eternal Spirit. All there is in heaven or on Earth is energy, thought, and form. Your full divine potential exists in the here and now, just as much as it exists in the highest heaven. God is here, too! There is no better place to be.

You can only begin this work; there is no end.

The Components
of Physical Immortality

THERE ARE THREE major components of physical immortality: the *philosophy* of physical immortality, the *psychology* of unraveling the death urge, and the *physiology* of physical immortality, which involves basic principles of body mastery.

The philosophy of physical immortality: There is a big difference between intellectual knowledge and knowledge that creates our physical reality—the theoretical and the causative. Intellectual knowledge becomes real knowledge through repetition and meditation. You haven't learned anything for which you don't have instant recall. We must master the words "physical immortality" like our own name. We must master the practices of earth, air, water, and fire like we have mastered driving, sleeping, and making love to truly be on the path to personal aliveness.

The idea of physical immortality gives people an opportunity to unravel their death urge and free themselves from the tyranny of deathist mentality. The ignorance of physical immortality leaves people in the prison of misery, self-destructiveness, fear, failure, and insecurity that causes illness and pain, violence and war, power struggles, impotence and cruelty, human degradation and death itself. The philosophy of physical immortality unshackles the human imagination, gives access to enormous reserves of energy and creativity, creates a motive for patience and simplicity, and is itself a test of love and intelligence.

The philosophy of physical immortality strips the mind of all kinds of fears and miseries. It permits love and divine energy to express themselves more fully in your personality. Therefore, even if you don't realize physical immortality, the philosophy is a wholesome group of ideas to work with and think about. In fact, the philosophy of physical immortality is fun and produces a more fun life even if it does not achieve the ultimate goal.

The belief that death is inevitable will kill you if nothing else does. But the truth is that your spirit is already eternal; you only have to move your mind and body into harmony with your eternal spirit. The philosophy of physical immortality gives your body a chance. Deathist mentality guarantees its destruction.

Death is a grave mistake.

The psychology of physical immortality: The difference between one person and another is primarily in the quality of ideas they think about. Thoughts of everlasting life produce health.

The belief that death is inevitable is unhealthy to humans. This is just common sense. Psychosomatic science has proven that our beliefs influence our health. So what practical value does believing in death have if you desire health? The belief that death is inevitable has probably killed more people than all other causes combined. Even if you survive old age, illness, and accidents, and practice the techniques of rebirthing and affirmation, your own belief in death will get you in the end— unless you change it. Seriously questioning the idea that death is inevitable is good and practical for both mental and physical health. Immortalists argue that if death really were inevitable and beyond your control, then believing in physical immortality wouldn't hurt you.

Perhaps our loyalty to death, or the "death urge," is a personality trait we could do without. The U.S. Constitution says we are innocent until proven guilty. Be immortal until you prove otherwise! Death is only an idle speculation as long as you are alive, but thinking about it may produce illness, failure, hate, depression, or helplessness when you could be enjoying life.

The death urge is a real psychic entity that can be isolated in your own mind and destroyed. Your death entity is composed of beliefs and ideas about death that you absorbed from your parents and culture. You can transmute this into aliveness simply by changing each negative belief into a positive one—one thought at a time. Use the affirmations technique. Instead of believing that you might die or be killed at any moment, simply affirm: "I am responsible for the fate of my physical body. Nothing can harm me without my consent." Just question death and the death urge starts to crumble!

In fact, it is very difficult to destroy your physical body. Your life urge, if you pay attention to it, warns you again and again, even before "accidents." Illness usually takes a long time to kill—plenty of warning to change your mind.

If your parents are not immortal yogis, the chances are you have a death urge. The death urge can be unlearned, but it takes wisdom and intuition, and lots of fire. Fire burns away the death urge and persistent negative emotions faster than anything. It is amazing how quickly sitting with a campfire or fireplace can transform a person from total depression to total joy.

The death urge is the most destructive of human emotions. It is responsible for self-sabotaging and suicidal behavior. The unconscious death urge is the stronghold for all depressions, sickness, and feelings of helplessness and failure. When you attack all of these things at their source (birth trauma, parental disapproval syndrome, unconscious death urge, past lives), it makes life a lot easier every day. And so it has enormous practical value.

We must unravel our death urge and become the master of all our conditioning. This normally takes fifty to a hundred years if we start early enough, because your death urge has a life urge. It will protect itself even at the expense of your body. Information on healing the death urge obviously should be available at all levels of public education.

Your body heals itself in accordance with your mind. Ultimately, it is only your personal connection to infinite being and infinite intelligence that will save you. You are an expression of all that is and are by nature eternal. Your death urge is self-destructive, and its power lasts only as long as you cling to it. The moment you let go of it, the eternity that is the fundamental quality of your being will manifest on a practical level as love, wisdom, joy, peace, and physical health. You can feel it expand with each positive thought! Let your body outlive your death urge! The death urge can be dissolved forever by consciously choosing the life of spirit, mind, and body, and the practical mastery of one's personal reality.

Dying is no way to live.

Perhaps you have practiced death long enough. You may have died a thousand times or more. Death is an austerity too. Why not abstain from death for a few centuries? It probably won't hurt you. To summarize, death is a bad habit, a useless custom.

Of course, it is OK for you to be another casualty in the universe again. But it is also a waste—a waste of divine bliss, of wisdom, of grace and divine beauty. The kingdom of God is not built by sluggards.

The physiology of physical immortality: The study of physical immortality—its philosophy and psychology—is nonsense without a complementary personal practice of spiritual purification that produces body mastery and happiness. Physical immortality may be as valuable to talk about as any other good idea, but obviously, talk without spiritual integrity is cheap. Without body mastery, this talk may lead to physical immortality in your next lifetime. On the other hand, even if it produces body and mind mastery in your tenth lifetime after this one, it may be worthwhile to work on in this one. Perhaps you have already been working toward physical immortality in previous lifetimes. Perhaps you will achieve it in this life. It is worth a try.

The physiology of physical immortality is based on inner awareness of our energy body. One must learn how to clean and balance this energy body on a daily basis with earth, air, water, and fire.

We also must master our physical body and its organs. We must become a healer who can heal oneself and one's friends. We cannot avoid diseases, but we can heal them. Each disease contains the healing process within it. Relaxation heals disease. And relaxation is automatically induced by mantra yoga and earth, air, water, and fire practices. Receiving massage is an earth method that always works to reduce disease.

The body is composed of earth, air, water, and fire. The simple spiritual purification practices with the elements form the basis of cleaning the energy body, maintaining the physical body, and mastering the physiology of physical immortality. Here is a practical thought: If your body works, don't fix it. As long as you are happy and healthy, you feel like living forever. When you lose it, you know you need to change your habits. Only you can unravel the mysteries of your own soul and body.

The human body is perishable but very dependable and miraculous. It will accept an amazing amount of abuse before it fails us. The moment we stop the abuse the body instantly begins to forgive us and heal itself. God's life and intelligence in our body is greater than our rational mind. That humans can die may be a greater miracle than physical immortality.

Put simply, the cause of death is really pollution in the body: physical pollution with food and toxins, and energy pollution through other people and our past accumulations. Both food and people are harmless in and of themselves, but it is possible to overdose. Sometimes overdose is obvious; sometimes it is very subtle. For example, it is possible to eat meat 25–50 years before it kills you through heart attack or cancer.

Getting rid of physical and energy body pollution faster than we take it in is what I call the spiritual purification game. The more we win this game on a daily basis, the more often we can live in the Spirit, and the more control we have over our lives. When we lose the spiritual purification game, we move towards aging and death.

Following is a concise list of steps that can double or triple your lifespan and enable you to maintain youthfulness, good health, and intelligence. Then you can decide to make it forever, if you like. Later chapters of this book provide more details on spiritual purification.

1. Master the practice of processing your thoughts and feelings to reduce negativity.

2. Master the practice of spiritual breathing and practice it daily—at least twenty breaths connecting the inhale to the exhale in a relaxed rhythm. This includes a consciousness of the energy body.

3. Learn water purification by daily bathing in warm or cold water and its significance in cleaning the energy body and unraveling birth trauma and womb consciousness. Meditating one hour per day in hot water can make anyone a spiritual master.

4. Sing the name of God daily: Om Namaha Shivai, or Jesus Christ, or Jehovah, etc. Master mantra yoga.

5. Develop a personal philosophy of physical immortality: eternal life of spirit, mind, and body.

6. Unravel your personal death urge absorbed from family tradition, past lives, culture, etc.

7. Practice three-day fasts a few times each year, and realize the truth about food and diets. Diet changes along with conscious bathing, breathing, fire purification, and an exercise system can heal most diseases.

8. Experiment with sleeping and not sleeping.

9. Participate in a spiritual community that practices all these ideas.

10. Learn to read emotional messages in body symptoms and how to process them with affirmations, breathing, and healthy practices.

11. Learn the role of exercise.

12. Study Herakhan Baba and other immortal masters.

If these ideas appeal to you, it is because you have grown up spiritually. You are ready for them. Take the exercises one at a time and you will find that they are easy for you. There is no hurry. The following chapters in this book provide more detail about these suggestions. But first, a little information about actual immortals and how I got involved in this fascinating study.

Immortal Yogis:
The Living Masters

MOST PEOPLE HAVE heard the words "immortal yogi" at some time in their lives. Very few people have ever met one. I took the time and trouble to find out if they really exist. It has been the most fascinating research of my life.

I have learned of many and met eight of them so far, both male and female. I set three hundred years as the minimum lifespan in the same physical body to quality for my research into this distinguished class of people. Three of these eight immortal yogis have maintained a local address on planet Earth for more than two thousand years. I met Ram and Sita one day in Holland. They come and go at will. I watched in amazement a relationship that has lasted for 130,000 years. They were totally into each other! There are *at least* a few thousand immortal yogis on Earth today. Most of them live in the Himalaya. A group of them always makes an appearance at the famed Kumbh Mela gathering in India.

The stereotype of the immortal yogi is a celibate hermit living in a cave. This is not always the case. There are female as well as male yogis (actually, the feminine form is "yogini"), and traditionally in the Indian scriptures, being a householder with wife and family is an acceptable path to total liberation and mastery. Shiva, Ram, Vasishtha, and Babaji in many immortal bodies have wives and children, for example.

The yogis who are completely committed to mastery improve their learning ability and accumulate greater powers every century. They reveal that practicing the Presence of God in truth, simplicity, and love is an eternal requirement for perpetual health and aliveness. But self-righteousness and unconsciousness can set in at any point, producing degradation and death. There are many ancient stories about this and the kind of character it takes to go the whole distance.

From what I have observed, eternal life is pleasurable. All the immortals I have met are having a great time. The science of everlasting life in the physical body is the science of enjoying life. Abundant life is the secret of eternal life. Personal aliveness is the source of joy forever.

One of the things that amazed me when I met these wise, simple, and illustrious people is that most of the other people who live near them—and we in the West, for that matter—have little or no interest in becoming immortal. This is still a great source of wonder for me. Is it a self-esteem problem? Gross materialism? Spiritual darkness of the human soul? Lack of imagination? Obviously, it is at least limited thinking, but why are people so limited in their estimation of human potential and in their idea of their own potential?

Yoga seems to be the only approach to life that produces immortal human beings. There is evidence that Moses, Elijah, and Jesus all studied with the immortals in India. When I read about these immortal beings in India, my first question was, "Are they still alive?" In 1977, I took my first trip to India to search for and meet immortal yogis. I didn't find one on my first trip but I did on my second. The first one that I met was Babaji of Herakhan, a Himalayan village across the river from Mt. Kailash, near Haldwani in the state of Uttar Pradesh. Mt.

Kailash is the historic home of Shiva Yogi—the Eternal Youth. Babaji is indeed this Eternal Youth. In the Bible he is called the Angel of the Lord. He is God the Father in human form. Later in this book I devote an entire chapter to this amazing being.

Jesus Christ is the best-known "immortal" in the West. Other saints have lived lives similar to Jesus. They conquered death and evolved to the point where they could dematerialize and rematerialize their bodies. They entered the other world without death. There is a way to get out of this universe alive.

Many Westerners attained these abilities. Analee Skarin of the United States did it in the 1960s. Saint Germain of France is the most famous. The saints are the source of religions, such as Jesus of the Christian faith. But we in the West are spiritually impoverished to the extent that we limit ourselves to the knowledge of the Biblical saints.

I used to believe that Jesus was the only one, but when I studied the facts, I was forced to change my position. Since meeting Babaji, I have come to realize that Babaji was an immortal long before Jesus and that he was a teacher and guide to Jesus.

The Bible presents to us five immortals: Enoch, Melchizedek, Moses, Elijah, and Jesus. The Bible specifically says that the last three fasted without food or water for forty days and nights. The Bible also tells us that all five of these men who conquered death had a serious interest in God. They are heroes in the Bible *because* they conquered physical death.

Elijah was the fire master of the Bible, as was revealed on Mount Carmel. He ascended into heaven without going through death. Ascending in a fiery chariot is symbolic of his lifestyle. When he returned seven hundred years later as John the Baptist, he majored in water purification. After his death as John, he was present with Moses at the transfiguration scene of Jesus.

Elijah was the fire master, but he lacked love and kindness

during his moment of glory so he murdered eight hundred men, women and children of the "false gods"—the other religions. When he reincarnated as John the Baptist centuries later, he was beheaded by his enemy to pay for this sin.

The lives of these immortals were devoted to God and based upon spiritual purification, which they learned from the immortal Babaji. But the Bible doesn't tell us the rules for eternal life, nor how to master the mind and body.... In fact, although the Bible holds eternal life as the goal of the Hebrew religion and the Christian life, it doesn't give us a clear idea how to achieve it. There are no immortal Christians in the most recent two thousand years of church history. The Christian church has produced the fewest immortals most probably because it is doctrine-oriented rather than life-oriented. The doctrine that the goal of life is to die and go to heaven stops all research. Such superficial doctrine is no substitute for the real godliness of practicing truth, simplicity, and love. Western science and philosophy are simply no match for the immortal yogi!

But there are indications that the ancient immortals of the Bible followed spiritual purification practices similar to what immortal yogis do today in order to gain liberation from the usual threat of death. Spiritual liberation and mastery really mean the same thing. It means to totally heal the emotional mind and thus to have a healthy body. It means eliminating victim consciousness and becoming the source of our goals and desires. It means to live in bliss, free of death as a necessity. It means to integrate spirit, mind, and body and have the ability to heal the body. Spiritual enlightenment begins with the realization that energy becomes what it thinks about!

Following is a short list of minimum requirements on the road to liberation and mastery.

- Choosing physical immortality: building a complete philosophy of life from the physical immortality perspective instead of the deathist perspective.
- Becoming aware of the energy body.
- Learning to clean the energy body with mantra, earth, air, water, fire, and love practices.
- Doing the spiritual purification practices for enough years to actually be ahead of the process such that you are healing emotional energy pollution faster than you are taking it on.
- Making peace with the guru principle. (A guru is an ordinary person who reminds people of their natural divinity. G-U-R-U = Gee, yoU aRe yoU!) See page 82.
- Choosing a lifestyle that supports spiritual growth and mastery.
- Becoming sophisticated in a knowledge of the great scriptures of all religions.
- Building spiritual community.
- Having a successful relationship with Babaji, the Eternal Father in human form.
- Unraveling the death urge you received from your family tradition.
- Healing the diseases of senility.
- Finding satisfaction in career, prosperity, and citizen responsibilities.

Eating of the Tree of Life, which means practicing the Presence of God, remains the Source of Eternal Life. God is the source of wisdom, peace, pleasure, mastery, materialization, and eternal life. Devotion to God is the source of the science of everlasting personal aliveness.

The choice to be an immortal yogi master makes you immortal in the present time. The trick is to stay immortal. This obviously involves mastering this choice in the Eternal Now. This is in harmony with our divine nature. We only have to remember, effortlessly and eternally, that we are the naturally divine children of God.

Beyond Senility and Aging

SINCE I BEGAN this work, I have learned of many and met at least eight immortal yogis personally, as I mentioned in the previous chapter. All the immortal yogis I have met are just living consciously and naturally. They illustrate that we can not only evolve our physical body into an immortal body of light that is indestructible, but we also can learn how to dematerialize and rematerialize the body like they do in "Star Trek" movies.

Physical immortality and transfiguration are the two basic paths of total victory over death. Ultimately, the human body is an energy system. I am convinced that people can dematerialize the human form by mastering the nature of the body as light. It is possible to go to heaven and back and to take your body with you. Analee Skarin says, "Death is the dreary back door into the other world, but there is a great front door of glory for those who overcome." The door between heaven and earth can swing both ways for people who are realizing their divine potential.

As for me, I healed the death urge I received from my parents in 1967. After doing this I experienced effortless success and happiness for fourteen years. I discovered rebirthing in

1974 and spread it, along with the idea of physical immortality, to hundreds of thousands of people all over the world by 1981. In that year, I had to heal the death urge again. This time I had relearned it from my students and it was ten times worse than the death urge I inherited from my parents. To make a long story short, it took me a year in the forest alone with the fire to heal the death urge this time. Since we can be reinjected with the death urge when we work in the world among mortals, we need to master the ability to heal it with fire purification and other methods.

After 1981, my life sailed effortlessly again until 1988. Between 1988 and 1993 I healed senility diseases, both mental and physical, which included eight terminal diseases such as cancer, arthritis, and diseases of the heart, digestive system, and liver.

To be mortal, we only need one terminal disease to give us an excuse to leave the body. To be immortal, we have to heal all the terminal diseases that are dealt to us by our family tradition, the karma of our soul, and our lifestyle. The idea of physical immortality is not to avoid the negative aspects of the human condition, like disease or aging, but to transform them. Each disease is a healing crisis that teaches us something. Every disease contains the secret of youthing. We may have an aging program in our family conditioning or a death urge, but we can outlive it.

We cannot suppress or deny our human conditioning, but we can release it. Superficial, positive thinking doesn't change body memories, but a healing crisis will. Mastering diseases and living through senility makes us earthy and practical. Metaphysics hasn't made anybody immortal. Yoga has.

The goal is to allow the human condition to teach us patience, wisdom, and compassion, not to pretend this human condition doesn't exist.

Healing Senility: Since senility, I have rebuilt my career as a teacher of spiritual purification, rebirthing, and the yoga of everlasting life. This has meant facing death over and over again as it confronts my students. Although it is much easier for me to do this than it is for my students, it is still life-threatening and hard work. I often feel like dying. Being a victim sometimes seems like a pleasure to me. But I have faced this mentality so many times that I am no longer fooled by it.

Aging and senility are the final exams of the human condition. You either pass or you pass away. Like me, you can become a senility graduate, but it takes the right actions and proper support. Mastering fire purification is basic to healing the senility diseases. (See Chapter 12.)

Most people don't survive. We can. We can live through senility and heal the disease of aging. But we must absorb enough physical immortality philosophy to have a motive, a reason. We must at least have the thought that it is possible. All the heroes of the Bible and the immortal yogis are here as encouragement. And all of life is an opportunity to prepare for senility. Overcoming senility is a critical aspect of the psychology of physical immortality.

Senility is one of the great natural barriers to total spiritual enlightenment. Senility is basically infancy consciousness. It is reliving in a psychophysical way the feelings and memories that are stored or stuck in the body. I refer not just to the complex physical organism we call a body, but also the spiritual body, the emotional body, and the energy body. The physical body is the embodiment of the soul. You can only separate these in your mind; they are one manifestation of Spirit.

Infancy is the cause of feelings of helplessness and hopelessness. We can't feed ourselves or wipe ourselves or even turn over under our own power for months. You can see this in convalescent hospitals. Senility is infancy consciousness in adults. Infancy consciousness is more significant than birth trauma.

Birth lasts only a few minutes or hours. Infancy lasts at least two years. Surviving infancy feelings is a full-time job. One has the deepest needs for sleep, touch, food, etc. Senility is a bunch of irreconcilable feelings. Beneath it all is the need for God— the Oneness of Eternal Spirit.

Once you are through senility and on the other side, life is profoundly different. You experience the promise of a lifetime of self-improvement. If you survive senility without dying, you will sense the spiritual liberation that lies ahead. You will taste freedom.

We are imprisoned by family and race conditioning until senility. Victory over senility consciousness is not only victory over death, but victory over conditioning. The body follows the liberated mind. Lifetime patterns of pain and restriction are released. Victory and mastery become natural.

Every layer of infancy consciousness released means a lighter energy body, more dependable mental and physical health, less struggle, less urgency, more completion, more order in one's life, more peaceful activities, less negative feedback from God and the world, more rapid manifestations. It means less dependency and less paranoia. This means more action and less complaining. There is more space in your mind every year, more peace, more free time, more leisure. It is not necessary to accomplish too much.

If senior citizens knew the spiritual healing power of fire, they could heal their senility diseases and become wise immortals and leaders of the community. Instead, most people are trained in victim consciousness and become useless, senile, old farts. I myself was a senile old fart. I plumbed the depths of senility misery, but thanks to what I learned about spiritual purification from the immortal yogis, I emerged victorious and became a senility graduate.

Senility can occur at any stage of life. No one believes in senility until it happens to them. Then they are usually too hopeless and helpless to care. Most people end up broke in a convalescent hospital, waiting to die. However, senility graduates can return to society as youthful, creative, and productive persons.

I believe that senior citizens who unravel their death urge will discover the fountain of youth within their own minds and bodies. The basic question is why they haven't discovered it already in sixty or seventy years. I believe the answer is to be found in the way children are treated in our society. Most people have experienced their divine child being suppressed at an early age. The natural divinity was beaten out of too many children. Children are not safe around adults who have a deathist mentality and who haven't unraveled the parental disapproval syndrome. Suppressing our natural divinity is so painful and takes so much effort that it leads to mental and physical illnesses and death. Death and doom are the final result of lying about our natural divinity. We are the glorious children of God whether we like it or not.

Senility is the process of rediscovering the natural divine child within. It is a natural form of primal therapy which begins the youthing process. This process can be started at any age. The technique is to relax into your thoughts of aging to let go of your fear of aging and its ugliness, and then to release the thoughts themselves.

Your natural divine perfection has a tendency to heal your emotions and body spontaneously when you release your negative thoughts. One of the natural qualities of Eternal Life and Spirit is youthfulness. You can fill your mind and body with youthfulness and health whenever you like. It is never too late. But it can feel like hard work.

Spiritual Purification:
The Essentials

MY OWN WORK and my relationship to living immortals revealed to me the full awareness of my energy body. The energy body is immortal. Without awareness of the energy body, which is a spiritual awareness, there is no motive to do the spiritual purification practices. A supreme secret to eternal life is cleaning the energy body, which is what spiritual purification is all about. The common methods of accomplishing this are not difficult, but simple and pleasurable. In fact, it is no accident that the secrets to eternal life are pleasurable and that the causes of death produce misery.

The reason there are so few immortal yogis is because people learn one or two spiritual disciplines and stop learning. This is a tragedy. God has an owner's manual for the human body and mind. The rules are built into nature. They are simple and obvious when you know them, but great mysteries when you don't.

Mantra (mind), earth (diet, exercise), air (conscious breathing), water (conscious bathing), fire, and love are the basic rules of the divine human owner's manual. Not much, but essential. But before I elaborate on the techniques of spiritual purification, let me briefly discuss the energy body.

Your physical body is created and maintained by wheels of energy, called *chakras* in the Sanskrit language. There are seven main wheels of energy, but every organ has chakras, and every atom is a wheel of energy. Our human body seen with spiritual eyes is like a solar system or a galaxy. An ordinary human body is a glorious miracle every day. It is much more than just flesh.

When a person is in the presence of another person, emotional energy is exchanged as the wheels of human auras penetrate one another. I call it emotional energy pollution. For example, vibes in airplanes are concentrated yuk. Typical symptoms from airplane journeys include digestive problems, headaches, depression, confusion, violent dreams, even suicidal tendencies.

Although airline personnel have it tough, the worst profession for heavy energy pollution is working in convalescent hospitals or with dying people. Many of the staff, even when young, die of the symptoms of the patients and/or grow old before their time.

We can sometimes take in either positive or negative seeds of energy and not feel a thing until later. Then we can be overwhelmed by them. Friends and lovers can wipe us out or make us unbelievably successful without our rational mind ever noticing the cause-and-effect relationship. To perceive and measure energy concentrations and the information they transmit is one of the jobs of enlightenment.

We need to choose to spend most of our time in a healthy environment and give ourselves adequate support. If we can find or create people around us who develop physical immortality philosophy and who practice spiritual purification, we can be immortal. Individuals believing in physical immortality who live in an environment of mortals usually die because they drown in mortal mentality. Conversely, mortals living in a community of immortals may live forever because they are nourished by immortal energy and immortal thoughts. Our choice of environment is very important.

Aging is created by aging consciousness, sickness by ignorance, and death by mortal consciousness. Our reality is created by our mind. Both the emotional mind and rational mind can be created and controlled by our environment. We have a tendency to become like the people we spend time with.

In addition to being aware of others' influence on our energy body, we need to practice spiritual purification daily to clean the energy body. When we win the game of cleaning our energy body we become healthier and more alive every year. When we lose this spiritual purification game, we become stiffer and more dead every year. Mastering life consists of the right habits and practicing the Presence of God.

Practicing the Presence of God means knowing that the Eternal Living Spirit or Energy is the source of your mind and body, even if you can't feel it. God is here with us even when we feel sick or lonely. Depression and anger, even lust and sin, cannot actually separate us from the Presence of God, but only make us *feel* like we are separated. As soon as we change the feeling (repentance), we can feel God again. When we are feeling God we feel love and peace, joy and harmony, inspiration, creativity, and wisdom.

This is why mantra yoga is so important. A mantra is a name of God. By continuously remembering and repeating a name of God (like "Aum Namaha Shivaiya," for example), we are using the power of words and thought to dissolve our ugly feeling and enable us to feel God.

Practicing the Presence means feeling peace and love and inspiration but also remembering and knowing with certainty that this Presence is with us even when we don't feel it.

A simple glance at the spiritual purification practices recommended in this book will reveal that they are main themes of the teaching of Jesus, the Bible, and all the great world religions. Practicing each of them in moderation evolves our humanity, as well as the divinity of all people.

The ongoing work of spiritual purification is called yoga. Yoga is the science of life. It is the science of God-realization. The yoga of physical immortality involves incorporating the basic elements of fire, water, air, and earth, as well as mind (mantra yoga), community (loving relationships and political responsibilities), and reverence for the saints.

My immortal yogi friends didn't give me the secrets of eternal life; they led me gradually into an inner realization of them. They taught me the rules of life and death by example. I can easily put them into words for you, but you can only know their meaning through practice and inner realization. The power of eternal life comes through repentance. You have to change your lifestyle. The following tools can show you how.

Below is a brief list; I will go into detail about each of these components.

1. Mind
   • Take charge of the quality of your thoughts.
   • Do mantra yoga and practice affirmations.
   • Spend time in meditation, analysis, and wonder *(raja yoga).*
   • Heal the emotional mind and your death urge.
   • Read the great literature and scriptures (the Word of God).
   • Choose life and personal practical aliveness over death.
   • Learn the power of devotion *(bhakti yoga).*

2. Air
   • Learn to breathe energy as well as air *(prana yoga).*
   • Master rebirthing (unraveling birth trauma and death urge, etc.).
   • Master alternate nostril breathing (see Chapter 11).

3. Fire
   - Learn fire purification and the fire ceremony.
   - Build fire into your daily life.
   - Remember that fire is as important to human health as food.

4. Water
   - Do *pranayama* in the bathtub.
   - Bathe twice a day.
   - Drink good water.
   - Learn the science of cleaning your energy body.
   - Achieve peace and relaxation.

5. Earth
   - Learn food mastery. How much does your body really need?
   - Realize that vegetarianism is a foundation for spiritual enlightenment.
   - Develop a personal exercise system.
   - Develop a divine career and live your divine gifts.
   - Engage in massage and bodywork, as well as playing percussion instruments.

6. People and Love
   - Be aware of emotional energy pollution and how to best process the energy of others.
   - Be part of a spiritual community.
   - Be part of local politics and neighborhood representation.
   - Revere and learn from spiritual teachers.

7. Grace
  • Learn the meaning of devotion.
  • Practice the Presence of God.
  • Don't just depend upon grace and ignore the rules!

These simple practices seem to be the rules built into nature that produce mind and body mastery. They are practiced by the immortal yogis. They naturally produce eternal life. It is necessary for everyone to learn to live on spiritual strength rather than mind power or body strength.

These practices give me a real feeling of body mastery. They are not superficial. They take practice and patience. Physical body mastery is not meaningful or permanent without the care and mastery of our energy body, which is the source of the physical body. Ultimate healing comes through awareness of the energy body.

Eternal life is consciousness in motion. Mind, energy, earth, air, water, and fire are the fundamental elements of consciousness, both divine and human. People become divine to the extent that they have a conscious relationship to earth, air, water, and fire, and of course to the God energy that is the source of all consciousness, life, and beings.

I will now go into a little detail about what I call the "Biggies of Spiritual Purification." These simple methods clean and balance the energy body. They are the eternal vehicles of grace, the secrets to health and aliveness of human beings. They inspire wisdom, peace, and even joy. They are the practices of all the world saviors.

The first four are air, fire, water, and earth. These are the physical qualities of God. They are eternal. They are always in motion and constantly changing form. They are both ordinary and miraculous. Using mind, earth, air, water, and fire all together gives you the world's most powerful healing tools. To know their secrets is to know the secrets of everlasting life.

Earth, air, water, and fire are great healing resources. Sitting with an open flame can heal all kinds of diseases; it is an ultimate healer. Some diseases can be healed most efficiently with water, some with breathing, some with fasting or right diet, some with mind techniques, and some with modern medicines. However, all healing is temporary until we heal death.

Air: Air purification means to consciously breathe energy as well as air—*pranayama.* The simple pranayama that I practice is the pranayama of newborn babies. Infants merge the inhale to the exhale in a continuous rhythm. This is the simplest and most natural pranayama of eternal life. Twenty connected breaths is a quick and tremendously valuable exercise that helps to clean the blood as well as the nervous system. Rebirthing is pranayama, or energy breathing, while relaxing; it is especially powerful when done in a warm bath. We can breathe away negative energy concentrations and clean ourselves inside and out with spiritual breathing.

Conscious breathing is a delight more satisfying than fine food.

I also practice three rounds of alternate nostril breathing per day as the pranayama Babaji taught me to keep my *nadis* clear. See Chapter 11 for more on breathing.

Fire: The example of the saddhus in India who live in a *dhuni* teaches us the value of fire purification. A dhuni is a small structure in which a sacramental fire is maintained twenty-four hours a day. When we sit or sleep near an open flame, the wheels of our energy body (our aura) turn through the flames and are cleaned. The emotional pollution of participating in the world is burned away. Death urges are dissolved by fire and water together as they clean and balance the energy body. Fire is as important as food.

Candles produce a beneficial result, but it is more subtle than from a large fire. The fire-walking movement offers a wonderful opportunity for initiation into fire purification.

Fire may be the highest element of God and requires the most intelligence to use. It is perhaps the most neglected natural divine element of God in our civilization. This neglect has put us on the brink of nuclear war. Nuclear war is involuntary fire purification for people who are not willing to do it consciously and voluntarily. The same technology that has moved our civilization away from the direct experience of fire threatens to bring us back in a few minutes through nuclear war. Central heating systems, electric stoves, and microwave ovens have moved direct contact with fire out of our daily lives. We should use our technology and wealth to build a fire temple in every park and neighborhood. It is critical that we reestablish the direct experience of fire in our religions and our civilization. See Chapter 12 for more on fire.

Water: Just about everyone in the West has indoor plumbing and hot water, making physical immortality available to the modern masses. As a result, it is easy for most people to bathe twice per day, as is the practice of the immortal yogis. I value hot water bathing as the supreme gift of spiritual civilization. I believe human lifespans have doubled in the last hundred years because indoor plumbing and warm water have made water purification so pleasurable. Warm water opens and cleans the chakras. Cold water cleans and automatically closes the chakras. These gifts of science and technology are worthless to us if we don't use them consciously.

Both showers and total immersion are necessary for the full understanding of water purification. Doing breathing exercises in the bath increases their efficiency. Oceans, rivers, lakes, and especially hot springs are infinitely valuable natural resources. Breathing in warm water produces different results than breathing in cold water.

The simple act of bathing daily in water can be a profound act of spiritual purification. To gain its full value, you should practice immersion in a bathtub, sea, or river while meditating before, during, and after. The value of thinking deeply while going in and out of water is that it enables you to discover how bathing changes your emotional and psychological states. Thinking while lying in a warm bathtub is the greatest form of meditation I have ever tried.

Daily bathing cleans the energy body. Drinking good water is also important, but bathing twice a day is the easiest and most pleasurable way to clean the energy body, which is the source of the physical body. To be immortal in today's world, we must learn how to soak.

Earth: Earth means movement, food mastery, and work. The disciplines of walking around your block once per day and fasting one day per week on liquids only may be all that is necessary to achieve perpetual longevity in the earth category. Most people die not from hunger but from overeating. Being a vegetarian is essential but not enough. Fasting one day per week on liquids—milk or juice first, and eventually only good water—is essential to clean the bloodstream and energy body. See Chapter 14 for more on fasting.

Earth purification involves finding work that you love and loving your work. Work is the supreme service to God, to people, and the secret to prosperity in the world. Prosperity means to produce ideas, goods, and services of value for others as well as ourselves. We receive money from others when we give them ideas, goods, and services that they are willing to pay for. A satisfying career taps the joys of our soul. It involves serving others in a way that covers our own life expenses.

Earth yoga also involves mastery of sleep. Sleep is a minor death—unconsciousness—that leads to the big sleep. Sleep is involuntary entrance into the astral world, as well as the suppression of unpleasant emotions. Eventually the body becomes such an unpleasant repository of suppression that we deposit it in the grave and escape permanently into sleep. But we get reborn, as you know. We can master sleep by staying awake all night during the full moon as often as possible, and by arising each day before sunrise.

Receiving massage and bodywork and listening to percussion are also forms of earth purification.

There are a few other important components of body/mind mastery, in addition to a conscious relationship with the above elements.

Mind: This aspect of yoga means taking charge of the quality of our thoughts. Mantra yoga is meditation on the name of God. You can use any name, but Babaji taught me that OM NAMAHA SHIVAIYA is the Maha Mantra. It is the name given to Moses in the burning bush and is common to many great religions of the world. In Hebrew it is "Om Shivaiya" pronounced backwards: "Ya Vah Shim Omen." The Catholic church changed "Omen" to "Amen." The Sanskrit is transliterated both as "Om" and "Aum." The idea is to clear our minds every day, to raise the quality of our thoughts and feelings. The Names of God constitute the fastest and easiest ways to realize our divine nature. Continual remembrance of God's name merges our consciousness with God; it is the supreme technique of aliveness and wisdom.

This is my steady diet. Reading the scriptures and other great spiritual literature also uplifts the quality of our thoughts. We need to heal our emotional mind even if it takes a century.

People and Love: The purpose of spiritual purification is to make us more wise and loving. Right relationships to people are the fastest way to total liberation. People can upset us and they can liberate us. Love is the secret of Eternal Life. Everlasting life has no value or joy without loving relationships.

Being a responsible citizen is also basic for democracy to work.

We must respect the immortal saints. We must find our true spiritual teachers and support them. They can teach us a lot. There are many truly great spiritual healers and gurus in the world today. Babaji is the source of all immortals and all forms of immortality. To meet him in his physical body is the greatest opportunity this world has to offer.

Grace: Grace is the lubricant for all of these spiritual purification practices. Grace, rest, and devotion are important to personal health and aliveness. Practicing the Presence of God may be the highest goal of the good life.

Grace is unpredictable because it is an expansion of the very personal God of the universe. The quantity and quality of the grace we receive for doing these practices is determined by our love for God and God's love for us. Our meditation on grace is the revelation of this personal relationship between us and God. Grace and spiritual purification constitute an eternal paradox.

Evidently energy breathing, vegetarianism, fasting, conscious breathing, a basic personal exercise system, fire purification, and other simple, pleasurable spiritual practices are the secrets to the victory over human misery and death. Spiritual practices daily clean one's sins and death urge. Mastery of the mind and body is so simple that we overlook the obvious in our mad rush for death and destruction.

Spiritual purification should not be used to punish yourself or others. To do it out of guilt or to prove something may make you into a fanatic, or an oddball. Master thinking, the practice of affirmations, breathing, and receiving massages first. Thinking, breathing, and touching can heal everything and make your life totally pleasurable and perfect. And chanting the name of God purifies all negativity and evokes all divine emotions.

All these techniques can increase the quality and quantity of your love. They can make you a warm, loving, and lovable person.

The Failure of Religion

P EOPLE ARE NO LONGER willing to allow their divinity to be suppressed by a religious inferiority complex that is founded in deathist mentality. Religions selling death and "pie in the sky by and by" have not created heaven on Earth. The fact is, heaven on Earth can be a practical reality.

The reason most religions have failed is because their goal is to reach fulfillment outside the body—through death. They have achieved their goal. The scriptures call the human body the temple of God. But if we don't find God here and now, death won't help. This means that the human body is the only true church. It is only by listening to the sermons in our own body that we can achieve eternal life. Unfortunately, it seems that people love their false religions more than the living temple of God; they value their bad habits more than their bodies.

As assemblies of people on the path of eternal life, Christian churches are supposed to be support communities. But two thousand years of history doesn't have a very high success rate. Orthodox Christianity today is a deathist religion. The reason the Christian approach to abortion doesn't work is because they decry the death of fetuses, while they sell death to adults.

Religious traditions that don't serve our personal aliveness are evil. Only by cleansing our temple of deathist tendencies with the breath of life and filling our minds with wholesome thoughts can we save ourselves. More people are realizing that the purpose of all scriptures is to teach us how death was created in human history, how to get rid of it, and the practical realization of eternal life.

Christianity is notable for its large gap between theory and reality. The doctrine that Jesus died for our sins makes a mockery of the truth about immortality. For example, Jesus taught, before his crucifixion, that his death would give his disciples physical immortality. He believed this because of the Jewish idea that people could sacrifice animals for their sins. He was raised in this religious tradition. However, he found through his own death that human sacrifice didn't work any better than animal sacrifice. Jesus discovered that no one can die for another and that no one can save another. Everyone has free will and must save or lose themselves. Yet in spite of the facts over the last two thousand years, the Christian church goes on teaching that the blood of Jesus saves us from sin and death. My study of the Bible, church history, and everyday observation teaches me that in two thousand years, no Christian has been liberated from sin or death because of the death of Jesus. This is simply theory. It is a false doctrine created by churchmen.

Why are Christians willing to settle for an easy answer when it doesn't work?

The death and resurrection of Jesus can inspire us to do it ourselves, but we need to learn how. The simple spiritual practices are the real secrets to eternal life. But the key is doing them, not just knowing about them. We must do these practices as long as we desire to be fully alive. The form of the universe and your body is maintained by habit. The only way you can stay the same person year after year is by returning to the same thoughts; habits of thought create us the way we are. The quality of these habits make us alive or dead.

I've been a born-again Christian for forty-three years and still love to meditate on the Bible every day, but believing in the blood of Jesus hasn't saved me from my sins nor death any more than simply believing in physical immortality did. Changing my thoughts and behavior removes sin. Cleaning my energy body removes the emotional and mental pollution that causes the diseases and death of the mind and body. Only yoga has a reliable track record of saving people from sin and death.

Although I have been saved and born again, I notice that I have to keep saving myself every day. Without daily spiritual purification I become miserable psychologically and my body collects pain.

The basic practices are built into nature and into your body and mind. They are detailed in Chapter 4. One can never "finish" with the practices—to stop growing spiritually is to contract and fossilize and die. Jesus did not stand for a pie-in-the-sky physical immortality, but for a physical immortality that you can enjoy in your body. As the Bible says, "The gift of eternal life may be yours."

Most Westerners don't know that Jesus is not the only ambassador of eternal life. Orthodox Hinduism records multiple incarnations of God. But Christians don't seem to want to know that God the Father incarnates as well as the Son. For example, they ignore the great Biblical immortal Melchizedek, who was also an incarnation of the Son. The Bible says, "Melchizedek was an immortal King at the time of Abraham who had neither birth nor death." The Book of Hebrews has five chapters about this great immortal. Jesus is called an immortal priest of the Most High God after the order of Melchizedek. Christians forget that not only Melchizedek but Elijah and Enoch conquered death too.

God in human form is more common in India than in the West, evidently because God took human form several times in India for thousands of years before the Western religions of Judaism, Christianity, and Islam were developed. God in human form in India is also thousands of years older than the Eastern religions of Hinduism, Jainism, Buddhism, etc.

It seems that Christians and Jews don't care about what God was doing before the Bible history—or after. Christians today have no ideas about the practical significance and spiritual practices that enabled Elijah, Melchizedek, and Enoch to ascend into heaven without going through physical death. It is common for orthodox Christians and "science-minded" skeptics to speak of Hindus and other Indians as dwelling in darkness and being in need of spiritual and material salvation. Meanwhile, immortal incarnations of God the Father are patiently liberating devotees from death—physical and otherwise—not only in India, but everywhere.

Orthodox, evangelical Christian doctrine and other systematic theological creeds try to put God in a neat little box of limited history and thought and to control it, or at least control people and the gates to heaven. My discussion of Jesus and Babaji is an attempt to show that neither Jesus nor Babaji fit into the little boxes that are constructed for them; both keep sneaking out of their theological boxes. Jesus would likely have the same problems today with the doctrines of men that he had two thousand years ago.

I am not trying to build a bigger or better box, only to illustrate that neither Jesus nor Babaji can fit into any doctrinal system devised by humans. All we can do is think about the knowledge we have available about these two immortals and wonder. No box, no book, no word is big enough to contain the mystery of these two people and the whole creation that they and we are part of.

The Death of Jesus Christ

I T TOOK ME twenty years to question the substitutionary atonement doctrine.

One day at church my preacher said to me as I was leaving, "You have to meditate on the blood of Jesus." So I decided to meditate on the death of Jesus Christ—what it means to me and to everyone.

The first thing I had to admit is that although it totally got my attention, inspired me, interested me in God and the Bible and religion, the blood of Jesus didn't change my life. The blood didn't get rid of my sins. It took hard work with self-improvement principles to get rid of every sin. Each change in my life has come from self-analysis, from changing my thought habits— and then my behavior changed automatically, when enough repetition and conscious reasoning moved my mind to a new space. Living life changed me more than the death of Jesus.

I get tremendous value from reading the Bible and sometimes from going to church, but I seem to get more spiritual value from soaking in my bathtub or being alone with my fire. Most churches seem to be filled with sick and dying people who aren't being healed by the blood of Christ or anybody. In fact, their doctrine seems to be a barrier to healing. In church

I may be lifted by the worship offered, but I am bombed out by the negative emotional energy pollution of the people. This teaches me that worship services are not enough, that individual spiritual practices on a daily basis are essential.

Secondly, I realized that the substitutionary atonement doctrine is based on the Hebrew practice of sacrificing animals on the altar to the fire as an atonement for sin. I can see how sacrificing my own favorite pet, sheep, or horse would stimulate an emotional catharsis, and I've done enough fire ceremonies offering fruits, grains, or ice cream to know that the fire ceremony works, no matter what you offer. But people don't generally sacrifice animals anymore as part of religious culture, and the idea of animal or human sacrifice (even if it were a special human) doesn't have the same value for people today as it had for the Hebrews two thousand years ago.

Thirdly, it was very noble of Jesus to die on the cross for other people's sins, but it didn't save his disciples and it hasn't saved Christians for two thousand years. The death of Jesus didn't take away my sin or death when I believed in it with all my heart, and I have yet to meet a Christian who is free of sin or death.

Therefore, the substitutionary atonement doctrine is a good idea, but it just doesn't work. It is a beautiful idea. I wanted to believe it; I did believe it for twenty years. I love the idea, but reality teaches us that we all have to heal ourselves and keep healthy, and that no one can die for us. Each person has to die for himself or herself, unless they learn how to ascend into heaven like Enoch, Melchizedek, Elijah, or the immortal yogis. Or they have to heal their emotional mind, learn how to eat from the Tree of Life, and master the body to conquer death.

Jesus got my attention and started me on the spiritual path, but my spiritual growth took a dramatic turn for the better when I met Babaji and I began practicing the simple purification disciplines with earth, air, water, and fire. Babaji is the

Eternal Father in human form whom Jesus addresses with the word "Abba" in the Lord's Prayer.

The supreme virtue of Jesus was that he loved Babaji and practiced the Presence of God. This is the supreme virtue of each of us. The Presence of God was available to me before I studied the Bible, and it is available to me and all of us forever. Christianity and other religions work to the extent that they tune us into God and have enough practical spiritual purification practices to keep us tuned in.

Fourthly, I decided to compare the teachings of Jesus himself about the cross before his death and after. Before his crucifixion Jesus told his disciples that his death would save people who believed in it. After the resurrection he told John and Peter how they were going to die. During this Biblical scene Jesus no longer has any illusions about the power of his death. When I realized this, I asked myself: If Jesus could know enough to see the future and tell them about their death, why couldn't he tell them how to avoid it? Obviously, he realized that the evolution of their soul in relation to their environment was not supportive of their victory over death, and he resigned himself to the contribution they were to make to history. He accepted their karma.

Why don't Bible scholars don't notice this discrepancy?

As I further studied the teachings of Jesus I realized that Jesus talked most frequently about *repentance* (the science of changing our mind) as the key to salvation. Jesus predicted his own death and resurrection, but he said little or nothing to support the Pauline doctrine of substitionary atonement.

Jesus said, "If any person keeps my saying, he or she will never see death!" What is his saying that gives us the power to conquer death? It is this: "No man can take my life from me, I lay it down of myself. I have the power to lay it down and I have the power to take it again. This commandment I have received of my Father." (John 10:18)

45

In modern English, Jesus is saying that physical death is optional. We are responsible for our own death. When we realize this is true, and we learn how to heal the body as Jesus and other immortals did and still do, we can also resurrect the body.

Jesus tells us that we can have this power by meditating on this thought until we have mastered it, and all our other thoughts are brought into harmony with it. This is what it means to realize our natural divinity.

Jesus tried to teach us that death has no power, except what we give to it. We create our own death out of ignorance. Jesus said over and over that he could do nothing without his Father's permission and power. This, of course, is true of everyone. God can interrupt our plans at any time and frequently does. That he allows us a huge margin for error, sin, and evil is a credit to his long suffering and patience. But it is not a credit to us, and eventually we receive due punishment. Physical death may be a merciful punishment in most cases.

Everyone who dies, dies for us, to teach us how death works so we don't have to do it—if we get the message. The Bible says, "God is not willing for any to perish, but that all should come to a knowledge of repentance." The knowledge of repentance is to understand how death works, how the simple practices of earth, air, water, and fire can clean and balance the energy body, and how essential mantra yoga and love are to our personal salvation.

The time wasn't right for the disciples of Jesus to become immortal, but the time is right for us. We have indoor plumbing and warm water for bathing. It is as easy for us to master our mind and body as it is for us to earn a living and support a family. We just have to value personal immortality as a goal.

Great Immortals of the East:
A Sampler

Babaji

MAHA AVATAR BABAJI is presently better known as Herakhan Baba, who dwells in the Himalaya near the city of Haldwani, northeast of Delhi. In spite of the glory of Babaji (which cannot be expressed in words), there are people in his village who have no concept of who he is. No doubt there are people who are born, live, and die within a mile of Babaji's residence and temple who have never seen him. Babaji can evidently put up with our ignorance forever without disturbing us with miracles.

The significance of Babaji, of God the Father in human form, throughout history is overwhelming for the enlightenment and welfare of all people. In addition to maintaining a local address and being available to people in conventional human form, Babaji has always appeared to people in dreams, in astral or psychic forms, and in physical form throughout the world and throughout all time.

I believe that Babaji has participated consciously in human history for millions of years. This immortal yogi master is the most intelligent and divine person I have ever met. In his ordinary-looking human form dwells the fullness of God in wisdom, power, and love. He is the embodiment of divine human perfection. He promises nothing but he delivers as much as a soul can receive and hold.

Babaji is the Eternal Spirit in human form. He is known as the Angel of the Lord in the Old Testament of the Bible. The Bible teaches that the Angel of the Lord is the Lord himself; he is God. (See Judges 13.) He is not like other angels—Michael, Gabriel, Lucifer, etc.—who are created. Babaji creates his own bodies and plays in the drama of his creation to improve the quality of human life. The words "messenger" and "angel" are some of the ways we try to refer to him because we cannot perceive the totality of his being. We can only perceive the existential message he is revealing to us. This spiritual education may be called the ultimate study.

Babaji is the source or inspiration for all religions. They are all attempts to understand him and to raise our consciousness to be like him. Babaji is Lord Shiva himself. "Shiva" is the Sanskrit word for God. Babaji is God the Father. *Baba* means "father." *Ji* means "supreme" or "respected ruler." There is always only one Babaji, but he has many bodies.

Shiva or God, the all-encompassing Spirit, existed before religions, before people, and before the creation. "Om Namaha Shivaiya" is the eternal name for God, according to Babaji himself. The first human form of Shiva on Earth was called Shiva and is portrayed in the Sanskrit scriptures as a simple yogi ascetic. His asceticism, however, encompassed all of life, including its pleasures. Shiva participated in everything, including abundant sex at times, but his predominant lifestyle was sitting alone in nature meditating, which he often did for centuries. Mount Kailash and Herakhan have always been his favorite places. He returns to this area millennium after millennium. He calls it the Supreme Universal Spiritual Pilgrimage. Today there is a beautiful ashram here. A constant flow of people visit it from all countries and all religions on Earth.

Shiva's garlands of snakes symbolize the basic principle of

the yoga of physical immortality. The cobra is a symbol for death. To decorate your body with death is to be the master of death. The awareness of the energy body and sensitivity to it is the secret to victory over death. Wearing death as a friend protects us from death. Our friend is nothing to be afraid of.

Babaji has appeared to people all over the world throughout all time. It was Babaji who appeared in human form to Adam and Eve, Enoch, Noah, Abraham, Moses, and the prophets. Babaji walks throughout the pages of most religious scriptures. His *Aarati* is sung throughout the world. *Aarati* means "festival of light." It is a basic worship service of divine songs that is sung daily. The *Aarati* is a powerful tool for self-healing. Every time I listen to it on tape my mind goes to the center of the universe and back.

Babaji is the creator and the director of his creation. When he is in a human body, he calls himself Bhole Baba, which means the "Simple Father." He normally lives such an ordinary life when he is in a human form that nobody can recognize him without his grace—in other words, through inner realization. He is not special, except to those who see. As Bhole Baba, he doesn't interfere. He waits for us to evolve enough to see him. He protects us with the minimum of intervention. He likes to see our responsibility and self-sufficiency.

Occasionally, he does acknowledge his true identity in public. He allows people to call him the Supreme Lord.

He can appear and disappear at will, which he seemed to do most of the time in Bible history. He has had innumerable bodies throughout the millions of years of human history. He often has more than one body at a time. Babaji is always active with us. He appears to thousands of people all over the world every day. Most of Babaji's extended tours on planet Earth seem to be in India, but some are in other countries. In 1977 Babaji appeared to a French priest fifty times and directed him to write a new scripture; it is called *The Revelation of Aires.*

From 1993 to 1995 he spent eighteen months in the United States. He published a beautiful and powerful book entitled *Herakhan Baba Speaks.*

Babaji is always playing with us in an attempt to improve the quality of human life. In his human form, he often benefits individuals without their knowing about it. It is a particular privilege to have a conscious relationship to Babaji and be able to recognize him when he serves us. This is most likely to happen when we are serving him or we are lost in the service of humanity. He is pleased when we become immortal yogi masters, but he also gives us the freedom and space to fail or to go through as many lifetimes as we may need to become an enlightened spiritual adult and a conscious spiritual master of life. The immortal masters almost have a doctrine against giving people too much in fear that they will take away the joy of discovery.

Watch for him to appear to you!

Babaji and Jesus

Jesus spent nine years in Benares, India, with Babaji during the missing years in the gospel record, between the ages of 12 and 30. Jesus learned his simple lifestyle and spiritual practices from Babaji at this time. A book entitled *Jesus Lived in India* gives the historical evidence for this. Jesus returned to Kashmir thirty or forty years after his resurrection, where he lived another thirty or forty years, then died and was buried there. An indigenous Christian church sprung up in Kashmir and has maintained his tomb as a holy spiritual pilgrimage site for 1900 years. This information is well-known in Muslim writings but has been suppressed in the Christian West until recent decades.

Jesus became a *saddhu* in India. A saddhu is a person who is seeking God full-time. Jesus is the most famous Western saddhu. You can see his simple saddhu lifestyle in the Bible, but not among Christians today in the West.

Babaji called Jesus to himself when he sent the three wise men from the East to the birth of Jesus. Giving us a clue is one of the ways that he works. When we search out the meaning of the clue, he rewards us with some spiritual gift or ability, or even himself.

After the resurrection, Babaji directed Jesus to work with the Essenes, which history reveals he did for about thirty years. Meanwhile, the disciples of Jesus were spreading his fame and message, which Babaji supported and participated in. The New Testament says that Babaji—the Angel of the Lord—was the one who released Peter from prison. Babaji took over the leadership of Christianity.

Although Jesus was resurrected from the dead, he was wounded not only physically but emotionally. Babaji encouraged Jesus to take a rest and to go to his next level in spiritual development. This would not have been possible for Jesus had he tried to direct the movement he started—the Christian church. Jesus and Babaji agreed that Jesus was to go into relative retirement and do his own spiritual work. During his time in Israel (about thirty or forty years after his resurrection), Jesus wrote *The Essene Gospel of Peace,* which is a marvelous work on spiritual purification. This gospel has been available to the church for 1900 years, but it has just been made available to the general public in the last century. You can order it in any good bookstore.

Babaji didn't require the death of Jesus to pay for our sins. His infinite mercy is enough, as God states over and over again in the Old Testament—as well as the New Testament and all other scriptures. God's mercy is not dependent upon human sacrifice, even the sacrifice of a special kind of human, as Christian doctrine asserts. Jesus died to work out his own karma and to reveal Babaji's glory in the resurrection. Everyone ultimately has to die for him- or herself, unless mastery is achieved.

The Old Testament, as well as Jesus and the New Testament,

say that Babaji is the only savior, but he uses Jesus and all of us in the salvation drama. Jesus deserves all the credit we can give him in our own salvation, but we have to save ourselves with the gifts and knowledge Babaji provides.

Jesus is one of Babaji's greatest devotees. I personally love Jesus even if he didn't die for me. I have an ongoing personal relationship to the living Jesus.

Babaji's Bodies

Babaji can create a human body directly out of Spirit with his mind. He can also come through birth and often does. He is always experimenting with the human condition. In his Krishna body five thousand years ago, he said to Arjuna, "We both have had many births. I remember them all; you do not."

The appearances of God in human form are called "theophanies." Babaji's bodies are also called *lelas,* which means "divine play." In some of these *lelas* he goes through death. In some of them he conquers death, sometimes repeatedly. Babaji can be either a mortal or an immortal yogi, depending upon what lessons he is trying to teach us.

One of the mysteries of Babaji's human body *lelas* is that he sometimes learns abilities in each body just as if he were not the total master of the universe. He allows himself to suffer all the mundane problems that we do, not only for decades, but sometimes for many centuries. It is like he is always in fellowship with us and testing the human adventure. He can step out of the drama at any time — as we can when we become spiritually enlightened — but he doesn't. He endures and lives out the human condition, experiencing in a human body even more misery than we can create for ourselves. It is amazing.

I wouldn't be able to write this unless I had met Babaji in several of his bodies and seen him actually doing this. However, in every body, his total transcendence and Divine Presence can be seen, if you can see it.

Babaji appeared to me for three minutes in Houston, Texas, in November 1977 and called me to India. I have visited him five times for one month each. My thought at the moment I saw him in Herakhan was, "This guy is either a nobody or greater than Jesus Christ." I totally forgot about this thought, but Babaji reminded me of it four years later. I noticed throughout our relationship that he could keep track of my thoughts better than I could. He does this for thousands of people—in fact, for everyone on Earth. This is how we can know he is God, not just a guru or an immortal yogi.

I am totally convinced that Herakhan Baba is the eternal Babaji known as the Yogi Christ of India in *Autobiography of a Yogi* by Paramahansa Yogananda. It is my great privilege and blessing to meet him in physical form and to be taught by him.

Babaji both dies consciously and achieves victory over death in all the methods. He personally plays all the games possible. He is the ultimate experimenter. Babaji is God in human form, but he is also the Eternal Infinite Spirit evenly distributed throughout time and space. We have to remember that when he is in a body, he is also inside of us and everything, and beyond all things.

Once a devotee asked him, "Are you God?" Babaji answered, "God is everywhere; I am local." This is the paradox of the bodies of God. He is in them and everywhere at the same time.

I am not telling you this so you will develop a belief system about Babaji or build a new religious organization (although one should be built). I'm telling you this to open your eyes, because as the Bible states, "Many have entertained angels without realizing it." Perhaps Babaji visits everyone at least once in a lifetime. If you recognize him or long for him, he may visit you more often.

When Babaji appeared to me and called me to Herakhan, he appeared in a different body than the one I met personally in India. It was a body he has deep in the Himalaya. So when I met him in Herakhan, I had to struggle from the very beginning with the idea that Babaji has more than one body on planet Earth at this time. Since then, he has appeared to me in various parts of the world in at least ten bodies, including animal bodies. Sometimes he will overshadow another body (such as birds and children) to deliver a message. Some of his bodies are materialized for a day, and some of them he lives in for a lifetime.

Therefore, seeking out and studying Babaji's theophanies in the scriptures, in literature, and in physical form is my first love. To learn from him and to practice what I learn is the source of my joy and aliveness. I sought Babaji to learn how to become an immortal yogi master. This is what he taught me. I still have a long way to go, learning the basics over and over until I master them.

Krishna, Goraknath, Vasishtha, Chaitanya Maha Prahu, and of course Herakhan Baba are among his more famous and recent bodies. As mentioned, Babaji is called "Abba" by Jesus in the Bible history; he is also called the Angel of the Lord in the Old Testament. In the Koran, he has more than one name. Khadir is his name in human form as the teacher of Moses. Allah is the basic Muslim name for God.

One body I'm focusing on now is Sita Ram Baba in Pokhara, Nepal. He is an obscure saddhu. I meet many saddhus, but they don't have Babaji's style and presence. This one does. This body appears to be about twenty-four years old, with a crippled leg. Because of this handicap, most of the people who accompanied me couldn't recognize him because they expected to see a rock star's model body and couldn't let go of that expectation. But for me he communicated very powerfully on the inside in ways only Babaji can do. He did this because I was open to seeing him in this form. I am willing to look beyond appearances.

Babaji had no beginning but many births. He never lost his divinity; he was a yogi master in his first lifetime and conquered death.

As yogi master, he has the ability to turn his body into light. He can dematerialize his body, go anywhere in the universe at the speed of thought, and rematerialize his physical body again wherever he chooses. He can direct the aging or youthing process. He has achieved the eternal life of his spirit, mind, and body. He is thousands of years old, yet his body stays young. He is richly human and ordinary as well as special, exalted, and divine. It seems necessary to experience him to benefit. My words are just not enough.

As mentioned, Babaji played in the human drama as Shiva, the yogi, for a few hundred thousand years. After Shiva, Babaji came as Ram. (It is a shame that so many Westerners are not only ignorant of stories of God the Father in human form that are found in Indian scriptures, but of the Bible stories as well.) Babaji had such great delight in his form as Ram that he also took his form as the Shiva yogi to see himself as Ram. After Ram, Babaji came as Krishna, a most powerful world savior who lived before the time of Moses and Abraham, about five thousand years ago.

Goraknath is a body of Babaji that has been well-documented in history for over a thousand years. (See Chapter 9.) His activities are often mentioned from before the time of Christ until AD 1200. As Goraknath, Babaji gave physical immortality to two kings in 57 BC. They are both alive and active in human history today. One is Gopchand, a king in Bengal. The other is Bhartriji, who maintains a simple temple and ashram in Bhartara, which is in Rajasthan. (See Chapter 8.) When Jesus visited Babaji, the latter was known as Munindra in Benares. Munindra ordained Jesus to be the Yogi King of the Jews. Moses and Elijah also came to see Babaji in Benares. During the last two centuries Babaji has been called principally by the names of Herakhan Baba and Brahmachari Baba. From the early 1800s to 1922, he spent most of his time in and around Herakhan village at the foot of Mount Kailash. This mountain is known as the holiest place on Earth.

From 1924 to 1958, he lived as a simple yogi in Dhanyon village near Almora, Uttar Pradesh. In this locality he also lived part of his time as Goraknath several centuries earlier. Goraknath is considered the principal god of the villagers in this area.

Babaji materialized his present body in adult form in a cave in 1970. He spent most of the year at his Herakhan ashram. He dematerialized his previous body in 1922. That is, he levitated and turned into light like Jesus did at his ascension after the resurrection. During his previous stay on Earth, he became known as Herakhan Baba, and it was while in this body that he initiated Lahiri Masaya into kriya yoga and therefore was made known to the Western world as Babaji, the Yogi Christ of India, in *Autobiography of a Yogi*.

I experience Babaji's humanity as more richly human than any other person I have ever met. And I experience his divinity as being in a class by itself, even though I know that he is only spirit, mind, and body like I am. I might say that his pure divinity makes him able to be human the way humans are really supposed to be.

At a certain level of spiritual development, people become aware of Babaji's physical body when he is in the world and are naturally attracted to him. To visit him is the ultimate pilgrimage. Babaji works silently most of the time. The fact that he is now willing to be visible and speak to the nations is a sign that people may be reaching spiritual maturity.

Whether as Shiva, Ram, Krishna, Goraknath, Munindra, Lama Baba, or any of his unrecognized millions of appearances, he uses the games of life to raise our consciousness and our enjoyment of spirit, mind, and body.

Babaji's Principles and Practices

Babaji maintains a very simple lifestyle. As the eternal Shiva
yogi master, he needs nothing. He can satisfy himself with his
own inner resources. He can manifest anything—food, earth,
air, water, the light and warmth of fire—directly out of infinite being with his thoughts. He doesn't need our gifts to him;
these are for our benefit. He doesn't need an ashram; it is for
us.

Babaji's principles and practices for achieving and maintaining physical immortality are simple and effective. Some
are listed below:

• *Sing the name of God.* Babaji recommends "Om Namaha
Shivaiya" as the eternal affirmation of your divinity. It is the
supreme name of God—the *maha mantra*. It evokes all divine
powers, wisdom, and emotions. The constant repetition of "Om
Namaha Shivaiya" evokes the presence, power, aliveness, and
energy of God in human consciousness. This chant can be done
twenty-four hours per day until it fills every breath and cell.
It can be done silently. If you prefer, you can chant Jesus Christ,
Jehovah, or any other name for God that evokes the divine
presence in your mind and body.

My favorite translation of *Om Namaha Shivaiya* is "Om,"
infinite being, "Namaha," infinite manifestation, and "Shivaiya,"
infinite intelligence." I like to think of God or Shiva as this
trinity of infinite being, intelligence, and manifestation. Infinite being is the eternal Spirit, divine substance, the Source,
the Father of the Christian Trinity, or the Mother or Feminine
Principle. Infinite intelligence is both creator and destroyer,
Thought, the Director of the power of being, the eternal begot-
ten Son of the Christian Trinity, the masculine seed that impregnates infinite being with content. Infinite intelligence is our
ever-present divine potential; every thought exists in the middle

of infinite being and intelligence. Infinite manifestation is the universe, the thoughts that stay there whether we are thinking them or not, earth, air, light, water, and fire, the Holy Spirit of the Trinity, God in action, the human body, the form of thought and being. It is not possible to represent Babaji without recommending this mantra and the practice of mantra yoga.

• Babaji constantly encourages me to *take more time to think and meditate.* He recommends that we devote several hours per day to pure thought. Clearing the mind and raising the quality of our thoughts is critical—more important than making money, to say the least. The mind is the source of a good life and healthy body. A person with a clear mind has harmonious and loving relationships. I manage to devote two or three hours per day to thinking, even during busy days, and this makes worldly success so much easier and more fun.

• Babaji calls breath mastery *mahayoga.* "Maha" means supreme or greatest; "yoga" means science of life or union with God. The basic breathing lesson is to connect the inhale to the exhale in a relaxed continuous rhythm. (See Chapter 11.)

• Babaji recommends carrying out several simple practices of *spiritual purification.* Part III details some of these practices; below is a brief summary.

Water: Babaji bathes twice per day in the Ganga River, which flows through Herakhan. In addition to cleaning the skin, water cleans the aura and balances energy centers.

Fire: He has a fire ceremony every morning in which he feeds the fire with grains, fruit, and butter. In addition, he has a fire pit in his bedroom that he normally sleeps next to.

Earth: Babaji recommends the mastery of food and sleep. Food mastery is achieved by simple diet changes. Vegetarianism is a simple path to fasting. Babaji also recommends walking, farming, and manual labor. He recommends that the divine person live in harmony with plants and animals.

Light: Babaji is well-known for shaving people's hair. During the spring of 1979, he shaved mine. Babaji also recommends that you develop a conscious relationship to the sun and moon. He says, "Staring at the moon all night can heal all the diseases of the mind and body. Watching the sun rise can give you cool strength that lasts all day."

Babaji is obviously the most adept psychoanalyst, with a cosmic and eternal perspective on each individual's personality. He can transform us rapidly if we are willing. If every person visited him in his physical body to receive his *darshan,* or divine glance, the realization of one human family would be inevitable. You don't even have to believe to see him. Sometimes the most ignorant and skeptical people have the most beautiful experiences with him.

Bhartriji

BHARTRIJI IS A YOGI, not a guru. He has maintained a local address on planet Earth for two thousand years. At this point in his personal development, he is a total master of his body. He can look old or young. He can adjust the age of his body as easily as we adjust the channel on our TV. He doesn't reincarnate; he has an immortal body that he has mastered. Yogis who achieve this level of mastery have an indestructible body of white light, but they appear ordinary to superficial observation. In fact, in studying any divine incarnation it is difficult to discriminate the ordinary from the miraculous. Ultimately there is no difference.

Bhartriji doesn't call people to himself like Babaji does. However, when people go to him for wisdom, he usually serves them in some way. The immortals teach by example, not by lectures. They view the mysteries of life as so simple and obvious that nothing needs to be said.

Bhartriji's ashram is located in the village of Bhartara (named after him) in the district of Alwar in the state of Rajasthan, India. It is on the road from New Delhi to Jaipur near a popular tourist destination named Sariska Forest Reserve. The forest reserve of one hundred square miles is actually Bhartriji's full home. He is the master of the environment, natural and human.

Bhartriji does a public demonstration of immortal yoga once every 108 years. The last one was 1898. The next one will be 2006. The demonstration consists of having himself buried alive and the tomb permanently encased in cement. Whether or not Bhartriji is dead is subject to the choice of the observer. Bhartriji doesn't care what you do with this demonstration. At his ashram are seven tombs, all intact, because he has done this demonstration every 108 years for the past 753 years. Perhaps this time Western scientists, scholars, and media will cover the event.

Immortal yogis like Bhartriji don't give philosophical or scientific explanations. They just do things and let us figure them out. I believe that Bhartriji teleports or dematerializes his body out of the tombs after they are sealed. Then he shows up 108 years later to keep his promise to do it again. Of course, this demonstration of immortal yoga is only entertainment unless it inspires us to practice yoga.

Jesus also did a public demonstration of immortal yoga through his death and resurrection. He said, "If they believe not Moses and the Prophets, neither will they believe though one rises from the dead." The Jesus demo has produced the same results for 2000 years as has Bhartriji's example and demos.

Usually Bhartriji is not available to the public between these demonstrations. As mentioned, he is a yogi, not a guru. Most of the time he lives his life for himself and for God, not for others.

I have learned a lot from Bhartriji. I have visited him four times: in 1981, 1985, 1989, and 1991. Because of Babaji's blessing, Bhartriji has always put in an appearance for me. (Also, Babaji told me I was Bhartriji's brother Vikram in his last family.) Each time I go to Bhartriji's ashram, I see more of him and learn more about myself and the infinite potentials of living. He is one of the true heroes of this planet. Bhartriji wrote many books 1700 years ago that are still in print and translated into English. Bhartriji, his writings, and his ashram are available to everyone.

During my 1989 India tour I met with a very great priest named Shastriji. It was he who first told me about Bhartriji. Shastriji said that Babaji had appeared to him in a dream and told him that I was Vikram, Bhartriji's brother. Shastriji gave me a book about Vikram, and of course I couldn't sleep until I had read it all.

Although I haven't had any past-life memories about being Vikram, it could explain my intense interest in Bhartriji. When I read books about Vikram, I instantly feel a complete oneness with the material. Vikram was into service in a way no other king I've ever read about was. This kind of service is the keynote of my life this time around.

Bhartriji is perhaps the easiest way for Westerners to study the immortal yogis. Every September, on the new moon, is a festival at Bhartriji's Sariska Ashram, attended by thousands of immortals and aspiring immortals. It is like a little Kumbh Mela for immortal saddhus.

The accommodations in the ashram itself are a little austere for most Westerners, but near the ashram is a Forest Service guesthouse with showers, and also nearby is a comfortable hotel called the Sariska Palace, which has bathtubs and hot water.

Bhartriji inhabits his ashram most of the time, but he can only be recognized by the lotus on his footprint, or if he desires you to know him. Even though he is elusive, he creates fantastic experiences for everyone who takes the time to visit his ashram with a sincere heart. He often appears to people in dreams while they are there, and sometimes he materializes and dematerializes in people's rooms. He also gives guidance to those who ask. He can give total enlightenment and immortality (God has given him this power), but few ask. If you go to his ashram you may have to master the grosser lessons built in there before he shows himself to you. Everyone who goes there will lose some of their superficial mind. This is guaranteed!

Bhartriji does accept students if they demonstrate enough endurance. If you dedicate yourself to Bhartriji for several years, or maybe a century or two, he might accept you. He is known to give his students many severe tests. As a result, he has few students. One I am aware of is a Supreme Court judge in Rajasthan; he is Shastriji's brother.

Bhartriji doesn't promise to be with you as Jesus did. But if you visit him, he will teach you so much so fast that your rational mind may take years to absorb it.

Bhartriji is a truly great yogi. He has gone for years if not centuries without food or water. This is not your average civilized Western lifestyle, to say the least. The culture of the immortals is beyond popular civilization.

Bhartriji's guru is Babaji in his Goraknath body. Goraknath has kept his body for more than nine thousand years. (See Chapter 9.)

Bhartriji's History (in brief)

Following the lives of immortal yogis can be confusing to mortal scholars until they open their minds to the reality of physical immortality. Most Western scholars have trouble dating Bhartriji and other immortals because there is so much evidence for their existence in different centuries that they feel there must be mistakes somewhere.

Bhartriji or Bhartrihari (also spelled Bhartariji) is one of the easiest immortals to trace through history. He is the most famous immortal I know about next to Babaji himself. I will tell you a little about Bhartriji, even if it sounds fantastic.

Bhartriji was born before Jesus Christ. Bhartri was his given

name. "Ji" means "ruler" or "mastery"; "hari" is a suffix given
to renunciates, meaning "pure and free of evil." Jesus Christ
and Bhartriji are contemporaries who illustrate two different
paths and styles of immortality. Jesus was a guru and a teacher;
Bhartriji had no public mission, perhaps because he was king
of all India before he became a yogi. Bhartrihari probably felt
that he completed his public service so he kept busy for several centuries meditating until he cleansed and mastered himself. Tradition says that Bhartriji meditated for seven hundred
years. It took him that long to figure out how to be the ultimate scientist—a master of the physical universe.

Bhartriji has more historical evidence of his physical presence than most immortals. He was emperor of all India just
before the time of Christ. He received physical immortality in
56 BC as a special gift and was enlightened later. His younger
brother Vikram took over the kingdom, and the Indian calendar today is measured by the reign of Vikram, just as the
Christian calendar is measured by the life of Jesus. It is interesting that the Christian calendar is measured by an immortal and the Indian calendar by a mortal, even though Vikram's
brother is immortal.

Bhartriji started out as king, but he has no interest in fame
or fortune. He has the greatest riches and power imaginable.
He has infinite spiritual riches in the kingdom of God. His
actual powers are far, far beyond science fiction, beyond your
imagination.

Bhartriji's personal history is similar to Buddha's in that
he was a king who gave up his kingdom to become a saddhu—
one who practices spiritual purification full time, sleeps on the
ground, and receives food and clothing as a beggar does, except
that they don't beg. In the beginning they may beg, but as soon
as their faith evolves to a certain point, they never do; they
only ask God, and if God and people don't offer them food,
they don't eat. Bhartriji is a master of transfiguration and food,

sleep, the elements, etc.

Bhartriji is different from Buddha in that he meditated for seven hundred years before becoming enlightened. Also, he started on the spiritual path much later in life than the Buddha did. And unlike the Buddha and Jesus, Bhartriji was never interested in becoming a spiritual teacher or guru and saving the world or his country. It was Bhartriji who said, "I am a yogi, not a guru."

When Bhartriji became immortal in 56 BC, he was emperor of all India. A good king, he was known for his honesty. Following is the story of how Bhartriji became immortal.

A yogi who worshipped the sun was given a fruit by the Goddess of the Sun as a reward for his austerities. This fruit had the power to bestow immortality. This yogi felt himself to be a simple man who did not need this fruit, so he decided to give it to Bhartriji, the honorable king of the land. Bhartriji loved his wife above all things and gave the fruit to her.

Bhartriji's wife was having a secret affair with the chief of police, whom she loved. She decided to give the fruit to him. He gave the fruit to his lover, who was a prostitute. She gave it to the man she loved, who was one of Bhartriji's ministers. The minister esteemed Bhartriji most in the world and gave the fruit to him.

A fruit with the power to bestow physical immortality is a very secret thing. Once eaten, it cannot be traced. And only other immortals will know that you have eaten it. All these people trusted the one they loved, gave the fruit as the supreme gift of love, and never expected the fruit to catch them in their dishonesty. Bhartriji was the only honest one in the bunch. Perhaps he was the most honest man in his kingdom.

Bhartriji was very surprised to get the fruit back. He thought his wife had eaten it. So he investigated and discovered the truth.

Bhartriji became deeply troubled. The two people he trusted

most in the world, his wife and his chief of police, had betrayed him. His disillusionment became so great that he left his kingdom and became a saddhu. He learned meditation, developed a conscious relationship to earth, air, water, and fire, and became a great yogi. He applied the same virtues to yoga that he practiced as a king. He became a king in the kingdom of God.

The spiritual purification practices of earth, air, water, and fire are so pervasive in saddhu culture in India that it may have taken Bhartriji seven hundred years to figure out the role they played in his immortality. It is obvious that the idea of physical immortality was implanted in his mind very strongly by the fruit. The fruit experience cost him his wife, his kingdom, everything. Bhartriji may have been guided unconsciously by God into physical immortality and the methods of earth, air, water, and fire. It took him seven hundred years to figure it out with his rational mind.

Spiritual purification is the ordinary path to physical immortality and transfiguration, but it is obvious that God can also use special techniques to save certain people. Bhartriji later met Babaji as Goraknath and realized that he was behind the fruit.

Bhartriji is the author of the *Bhartrihari Shatkam,* a milestone of human literature, written when he was only 300. At this age he survived senility, although he wasn't yet enlightened. These verses are seasoned wisdom. The *Shatkam* has been a classic piece of literature in Hindu and Buddhist culture for more than 1500 years. It has been used in the official training of Buddhist monks for 1700 years, the only non-Buddhist book to be used in such training. Bhartriji wrote other books on Sanskrit grammar, epistemology, and the science of mastering time. His epistemology—the science of how our ideas relate to their objects—is considered by many Western scholars to be the best in the world. These books are available in English.

As we grow to enlightenment, life becomes more simple. The secrets of life and the universe become obvious. One of the reasons the great immortals don't lecture is because our confused minds become a mystery to them. They can no longer understand how we overlook the obvious day after day. God is so ordinary that nobody notices him. All the great divine powers are simple and obvious once we have mastered them. Walking on water is as easy as driving a car after we learn it. Physical immortality is natural. It is death that is unnatural to our divine nature.

If you'd like Bhartriji's guidance you can work with this mantra: *Om Bhartriji Jai Shree Bhartriji.*

Goraknath

NINE THOUSAND YEARS AGO, the Lord of the Universe, the Eternal God, or whatever you want to call him or her, decided to incarnate in a human body. It wasn't the first time.

He chose the body of a dead baby that had been thrown on a city garbage dump. The baby was alive when it was thrown there, but it died of starvation and exposure. This was the cruel form of infanticide that was used when humans began their most recent degradation 9000 years ago.

"Nath" means "Lord," and "gorak" means "garbage." Goraknath is the Lord of Garbage. The Eternal Father began this incarnation as Goraknath 3000 years before Adam and Eve, who are dated at 4000 BC. The Bible records the descent of humanity into death.

The great scriptures that precede Bible history tell us that human lifespans were once much longer. According to the *Ramayana*, Ram and Sita lived more than 10,000 years. This was about 130,000 years ago. They established a period when physical death was optional. The Bible history records the end of this last great period of physical immortality (about 6000 years ago), when lifespans were still 500 to 1000 years. Adam died at 930 years. The Bible records the descent of humanity into death.

The Bible says that human lifespans were reduced to 120 years about 4500 years ago—at the time of Noah—because the thoughts of our hearts became only evil continually (Genesis 6:5). Later, at the time of Moses roughly 3500 years ago, human lifespans were reduced to 70 years. Today they are expanding again as we enter the New Age of physical immortality. Working behind the scenes, Babaji in his various bodies such as Goraknath has been systematically, gradually, and very thoroughly building life-support systems into our civilization to realize this new age of enlightenment and immortality.

The oldest and grandest scriptures are the *Shiva Purana,* written millions of years ago and recording millions of years of human history. The *Shiva Purana* promises the incarnation of God the Father to save humanity during our time today. Goraknath is a fulfillment of this prophecy made millions of years ago. "Shiva" is the eternal name of God. Shiva promised to return in human form for the salvation of humanity during this time, which is called the Kali Yuga. "Kali" means "darkness," and "yuga" means "era or period." Kali Yuga refers to the rule of evil, when people's minds are ruled by time, limitation, or materialism. A kali yogi is a destroyer of evil or time.

God incarnated as Goraknath 9000 years ago and has maintained a physical body on Earth the entire time. He is the great Kali Yogi—the destroyer of time, limitation, evil, and death. He is the bringer of truth, simplicity, love, and immortality.

Actually, as I've said repeatedly in these pages, it is my belief and experience that God the Father has incarnated millions of times and that he appears to millions of people every day all over the world. God is alive and well in the 1990s.

God took the body of the dead baby on the garbage heap to awaken perverted humanity out of its slumber in time and materialism, which the *Shiva Purana* says is the most dangerous period in all human history for the spiritual well-being of the human soul and body. It is spiritually dangerous because material comfort makes life so easy that people forget God. Then the death urge becomes stronger, and mass destruction is caused by unenlightened people loaded down with death urge. People become zombies without love or aliveness. Peace, wisdom, and joy are forgotten and no longer valued as much as money.

Goraknath has trained more immortal humans in the last 100,000 years than anyone since Ram and Sita. The Lord of Garbage is redeeming materialism, you might say.

In India it is traditional for gurus to give food to their disciples—it is called *prasad,* which means holy food. Goraknath is famous for sweeping the streets and serving garbage as prasad. The lessons in this practice are endless. The Bible says God exalts the base things of this world to confound the wise and the proud (today we might say "the civilized"). Jesus brought the practice of giving prasad from India into Christianity, where it is called communion. The stories throughout the 9000 years of Goraknath's history are endless. Yet orthodox Christianity has managed to keep the Western world totally ignorant of Goraknath.

The basic style of God the Father in human history is to live as a simple yogi. He teaches truth, simplicity, and love by example. He is available to all, but few seek him out.

Goraknath lives in the world for a few decades, absorbing the karma of his disciples into his own body. Then he disappears into the Himalaya for a few decades to do spiritual purification—setting an example for us. He heals and rejuvenates his body and comes back again to participate in the world.

The people who draw close to him learn as much as they can hold in each lifetime. They meet him lifetime after lifetime until they also become like the Eternal Youth and become immortal. They integrate spirit, mind, and body. They learn to live truth, simplicity, and love.

In Kathmandu, Nepal, there is a Goraknath Temple that was built in one night. Beside this temple is a *dhuni,* a little house with a sacred fire in it. (See Chapter 12 for more about dhunis.) This fire has been burning for more than a thousand years. It has been continuously manned by Goraknath devotees. There are about 100 million people in Goraknath religions on the subcontinent today.

Near this temple in Kathmandu is a miraculous tree. Goraknath blessed this tree a thousand years ago. Since then, every autumn this tree rains blossoms from 4 AM to 4 PM. Many poor people gather the blossoms of this holy tree and sell them in the market. This tree keeps many people from starving. It is a great teacher. It just sits there manifesting God's beauty, love, and prosperity every day during its season, century after century. Western philosophy is no match for the immortal yogi who can bless a tree and thereby feed and inspire people for centuries. Goraknath is the largest influence in the spiritual evolution of planet Earth for the last ninety centuries, and most Westerners have never heard his name.

I have met disciples of Goraknath who are 300 years old and 2000 years old. Bhartriji is a disciple of Goraknath. I have only just begun to research the many books about Goraknath. Only a few are in English. It seems there is no market for this information in the modern Christian world.

Goraknath is a savior of the world. He is patiently directing the evolution of governments, science, technology, education, and religions to induce enlightenment and democracy. God the Father, visible and invisible, omnipresent and embodied, is leading the spiritual evolution of the individual into total liberation of spirit, mind, and body. He is not competing with Jesus; Jesus is helping him. They both continue to participate in human history. But we need to remember that God the Father has many bodies and many historical identities. His names during a particular century often reflect his lifestyle or the locality where he lives. During the last millennium Babaji was known as Lama Baba in Tibet, Chitanya Maha Prabhu in central India, Babaji Nataraj in southern India, and Haidakhan Baba in the lower Himalaya. He is best known as Haidakhan Baba in the last century.

God the Father has appeared to me in many different human bodies, animal bodies, and other forms (as he did to Moses) to deliver different messages. At a certain point in your relationship you can tell the difference, and at another point there is no difference. He is everywhere. He is a particular historical person, and he is omnipresent.

I am not unique. God/Goraknath/Babaji plays with anyone who is willing to play. He will play with you when you are ready. You probably are or you wouldn't have gotten this far in this book. God the Father can have a personal relationship to every person on Earth. Think about it!

Immortality—The Stages of Mastery

A Summary of Information in This Book

A S REVEALED BY the immortal yogis such as the ones you
have just read about, spiritual practices are the eternal
vehicles of grace. They are not dependent upon the doctrines of men nor the beliefs of the church; they work for everyone of all faiths and no faith. They are scientific. A shower
always makes me feel better whether I believe in it or not.
Fasting always heals and makes me feel better. I don't have to
believe in it. Connected breathing and fire always produce
results. Every year that we do spiritual practices our body
becomes lighter, healthier, and more obedient. Eventually mastery is inevitable, whether it takes us a hundred years or five
hundred years or many lifetimes. Mastery is the sweetest
reward. By definition, it includes everything!

Mastery means to eliminate victim consciousness and to be
the cause of our goals and desires. It means to live in bliss, except
when consciously healing someone in pain. It means to be free
of death as a necessity. It means to integrate spirit, mind, and
body, and to have the ability to heal the body. It means to heal
the emotional mind and be a conscious master of our feelings.
It means to prefer spiritual pleasures over physical pleasures,
but the true pleasure of physical pleasure is spiritual—the spir-

itual quality or dimension of them. And most physical pleasures are legitimate for immortals and harmless. In fact, most
evils by themselves are relatively harmless; it is when we turn
them into habits that they become destructive. When our life
energy is controlled by evil habits, the evil habits destroy us by
destroying our will to live. Even some good habits can kill us
when we are ruled by the habit instead of ruling it. We destroy
our body by lack of respect for it as our personal divine gift
from God. The physical body is our most valuable possession,
but people sacrifice it to win the money game, to support their
car or house, or to please their friends or their deathist religion.

Without spiritual purification practices, our body becomes
heavier every year, diseases become more common, and death
is inevitable. You don't have to wait to die and go to hell to be
miserable. You only have to neglect spiritual purification and
live an unbalanced and undisciplined life. Spiritual practices
are more important for personal mastery than knowledge. We
become jaded when we learn more and more self-improvement techniques that we don't practice.

Living consciously means to progress naturally through the
stages of mastery. Eventually all the organs and abilities of the
body will become a part of our conscious mastery. We are naturally divine now. Holding our divinity in mind, we can enjoy
the ordinary games of human existence while we are developing the stages of spiritual mastery. Achieving excellence in
these games is part of self-mastery and healing.

1. Choosing physical immortality is level one. It involves
building a complete philosophy of life from the physical immortality perspective instead of the deathist perspective. Such thoughts move us in the right direction,
but we must produce the right actions to create results.
The widely available *Science and Health* by Mary Baker
Eddy is a massive contribution to immortal thinking.

2. Become aware of the energy body—a major stage toward mastery.

3. Learn to clean the energy body with mantra, earth, air, water, fire practices, and love practices. There is no substitute for this. These rituals are all very pleasurable to do and create a life of satisfaction and spiritual mastery. They keep our mind and body tuned into the Presence of God, which is the experience of ecstasy.

4. Do the practices for enough years to actually be ahead of the spiritual purification process, so that you are healing emotional energy pollution faster than you are taking it on. Participation in the world of mortals does have a cost. I call it emotional energy pollution. We have to win the game of spiritual purification.

5. Make peace with the guru principle—internal and external discipline. We may need a teacher. (See page 82.)

6. Choose a lifestyle that supports spiritual growth and mastery. We may need more solitude!

7. Become sophisticated in a knowledge of the great scriptures of all religions and the great human literature, especially the *Shiva Purana.* The Bible contains the case histories of five immortals, plus Babaji—the Angel of the Lord. The *Shiva Purana* contains case histories of thousands of immortals. It contains the most sophisticated story of Creation.

8. Build spiritual community as a personal support environment for our collective healing and physical survival. Churches only work if they are based upon spiritual practices. Most people in most churches are sick and dying like everyone else. Breathwork and spiritual practices with fire, fasting, etc., are the source of the true

revival the Christian church is seeking.

9. Find satisfaction in career, prosperity, and citizen responsibilities. Choose a career that supports our aliveness and is not too costly from the standpoint of emotional energy pollution. One's career must have a proper balance between solitude and participation—between meditation and worship and worldly success. Spiritual purification is more important than money. And it supplies us with the energy and wisdom to achieve great success. Jesus was right when he said, "Seek first the Kingdom of God and His righteousness, and all material things will be effortlessly and joyfully added to you."

10. Have a successful relationship with Babaji, the Eternal Father in human form, and make him available to your friends on this path. He usually has at least one body on the planet at all times. God, the Eternal Father-Mother, has not stopped revealing Himself-Herself. They are participating in history today and appear to thousands of people magically every day. They are willing to play with you! Open your mind!

11. Unravel the death urge you received from your family tradition. This is easy for some and difficult for others. Some people can't even feel the death urge until their parents die. But what if your parents become immortal and don't die?

12. Heal the diseases of senility. Senility is the final exam to the human condition, a major barrier to physical immortality. Most people give up and die rather than go for personal mastery. We would rather let someone else do it for us. This is where we have to master helplessness, hopelessness, infancy consciousness, birth trauma, womb consciousness, etc. You must know that it is possible to

live through and heal all the popular terminal diseases of senility. One of the reasons Christianity doesn't work is because it still preaches welfare salvation. Repentance (which Jesus preached) works better—repentance means the science of changing one's mind.

13. Actually heal birth trauma, womb and infancy consciousness, the parental disapproval syndrome, and the unconscious death urge from family and past lives, and consciously use the power of the human mind. Healing the emotional mind is our main job in our first century.

14. Shiva Kalpa is the basic rite of rejuvenation—a twelve-year course.

The above all relate to mastery of the human condition; next comes our divine potential.

15. Learn transfiguration—dematerializing and rematerializing the body at will.

16. Experiment with teleportation, astral projection, levitation, walking on water, etc. These skills are attained after we become a loving and enlightened humanitarian. They are less important than being a fully participating citizen.

17. Master food, sleep, and sex. The forty-day fast (no food or water) was a common denominator of immortals in the Bible. Mastering food seems to have something to do with mastering the body and death. This is obvious if you think about it.

18. Develop a conscious relationship to the sun, moon, planet Earth and its ecology, etc. The scriptures of the immortal yogis have much to teach us about this.

19. Master the body organs instead of being controlled by them.

20. Be able to heal the body and make it invincible to wounds, diseases, and death, even bullets.

21. Master the million yogas that it takes to build a human body directly out of spirit with the mind. Evolution can begin at any point and proceed in any direction. We are wholly the Eternal Spirit right now—body, atoms, and cells included.

The Guru Principle

I didn't want to interrupt my list, but I would like to elaborate a bit on this point. Shiva defines "guru" as the conscious self of every person. The guru is our personal connection to Infinite Intelligence. Yet some people have developed this connection more than others, and these enlightened people can tune in for us or tune us in to get excellent divine guidance.

Selecting a person to be our guru or spiritual teacher means that we allow them to provide external guidance or discipline until we master certain principles. For example, I often guide people's diet until they get a healing. Or I select a specific program for breathing or for fire purification.

I studied with immortal yogis until I had my own inner realizations of what it is about. I received these realizations through the practices they patiently taught me. It took several years for me to master my energy body in relation to the basic practices. I still have a lot to learn. My relationship to Babaji as my guru is an external relationship that has been going on for many lifetimes.

Suggested Practices for
Spiritual Purification

Spiritual Breathing

MASTERING THE BREATH of life is the key to spiritual, mental, and physical health. Breath mastery is the ultimate spiritual mastery. In the Bible, breath mastery is called "eating the Tree of Life." In yoga, breath mastery is called *maha yoga*—the supreme science of life. The mind and the breath are the king and queen of human consciousness. The breath is the power and the mind the director of this power.

It is amazing that people in our society can get a college degree without learning how to breathe. The rebirthing movement is dedicated to making breath mastery as common as eating and sleeping. We believe that in the not-too-distant future spiritual breathing will become more popular than sex is now. Those who have mastered the breath experience enjoy spiritual breathing as much if not more than sex because it is a biological experience of God, and it produces physical and emotional satisfaction with every breath.

Rebirthing is an American form of prana yoga that is closest to kriya yoga. It may be called scientific breathing rhythm, spiritual breathing, or intuitive breathing. It is a psychophysical experience of Infinite Being whereby one connects the inhale with the exhale in a relaxed, intuitive rhythm until the inner breath, which is the spirit and source of breath itself, is merged with air, the outer breath. As the inhale and exhale are merged, a vibrating sensation is activated in the body which increases in intensity until the whole body is immersed in divine energy flows. These vibrations pass through the nervous and circulatory systems, cleansing psychic dirt, tension, and illness out of the mind and body. A cycle is complete when the vibrations stop, leaving calm in their wake.

Relaxing on the inhale is the key to relaxing on the exhale. Relaxing so that gravity does the exhaling preserves twice as much energy for the next inhale. Rebirthing merges spirit and matter in a simple, scientific method of spiritual breathing. Unity of inhale and exhale is the physical experience of the unity of being—oneness with God.

Rebirthing is something special. It is the power of God for the salvation of the body and cleansing of the mind. Rebirthing is a method of spiritual breathing that in just a few minutes produces the most profound religious experience.

This direct, intuitive experience of God through the human breath is very fast and very deep. The breath of life has always been one of the simplest, most direct, and powerful methods of spiritual purification. The breath of life can send mind and body on a trip through the cosmos. Connecting the inhale to the exhale in a relaxed rhythm brings about an awareness of a direct mental perception of spirit, and a physical sensation of the actual life energy.

Intuitive breathing (rebirthing) routinely heals asthma, migraines, epilepsy, the common cold, and many other diseases too numerous to list. The chief value of intuitive breathing is healing the tension and pain we collect in everyday life. These ordinary stresses, strains, and traumas encountered in the process of working and living tend to inhibit our breathing ability. Intuitive breathing has a role to play in healing almost every disease because breathing is fundamental to human existence.

I could relate thousands of cases of healing and list the hundreds of diseases that have been healed, but it is useless because other people's healing doesn't do you any good. It has to happen to you.

Learning intuitive breathing or rebirthing is the best thing we can do for ourselves. This ability dramatically improves our health, happiness, and success. Intuitive breathing is a self-healing skill we can use every day to renew mind and body with fresh life energy.

Regardless of how salubrious intuitive breathing is, the benefits can be overwhelmed by poor diet and an undisciplined lifestyle. Conscious energy breathing is essential for self-healing, but it is only one tool and must be supplemented with good diet, regular fasting, exercise, daily bathing, fire purification, and wholesome thoughts and feelings.

A rebirther is a breathing guide who has practiced enough to initiate another person into this awareness. The purpose of having a rebirther is to maintain a safe, supportive environment and to guide the person's breathing rhythm until the session is complete. It normally takes a rebirther five to ten minutes to guide a person into a rhythm that is free and relaxed enough to perceive God in mind and body. The rebirthee normally experiences a profound sense of inner cleanliness and divine feelings of love and serenity.

The rebirthing session may contain dramatic emotional or physical changes, which are sometimes labeled by the medical community as the hyperventilation syndrome. Actually, spirit is cleaning, balancing, and nourishing the human mind and body. Kriya yoga was a nineteenth-century form of intuitive breathing, dispensing this power of breath in a tight set of disciplinary practices, for the purpose of protecting people from the dramatic physical and emotional changes that the power produces in human personalities as it purifies—the changes that are generally called the hyperventilation syndrome.

The goal is to connect the inhale to the exhale for at least one hour per day. It is recommended that people who begin this practice without the personal instruction of a rebirther limit themselves to twenty connected breaths once or twice per day. This recommendation is based upon the possibility of experiencing the hyperventilation syndrome without proper preparation.

Some people master this simple breathing lesson quite easily; others seem to have great difficulty. The basic difference seems to be the quality and quantity of psychological trauma that a person has accumulated before they begin learning this simple breathing lesson. This trauma might be categorized into birth, parental conditioning, death urge, and misuse of the power of the human mind. Some people would add karma from previous lives. The hyperventilation phenomenon is viewed by rebirthers mostly as birth trauma. Hyperventilation is a natural healing process by which the breathing mechanism is freed from the inhibitions placed on it while learning to breathe in a tense and fearful atmosphere during birth. It is caused by primal fear.

Another common dramatic physical manifestation of the "hyperventilation syndrome" is called tetany by doctors. The theory of rebirthing and ancient yogic science about this phenomenon of locked jaws and muscles is that the divine energy is cleaning the physical body of past fear. Such dramatic symptoms only occur when a person's mind is ruled by fear. Usually, it is the memory of the fear of being born—the emotional memory of contractions. It can also be tension caused by emotional energy pollution accumulated during any period of life.

Some people fear their own breath. And some people fear their own Life Force, especially when it flows in their body physiologically in powerful ways. Fear causes constriction and tension. Intense tension we call pain. Tetany is the physical manifestation of this fear during breathing sessions. It is possible to develop a fear of tetany.

It is common for some people to experience some tetany in one to three breathing sessions. A few personalities who have chronic fear from birth trauma or other experiences may be troubled by tetany for more than three sessions. The paradox is that people who are openly fearful usually don't have much trouble with tetany. It is the people who have their fear totally suppressed and don't believe they have any fear who have trouble with tetany.

Tetany is a cramping or paralysis of the fingers or other extremities that normally disappears after a few more minutes of connected breathing. It is valuable to know about it before your first connected breathing session so that you are not surprised by it and can more easily breathe it away. You cannot have tetany and relaxation at the same time. If you continue the connected breathing, deeper relaxation occurs because every inhale and every exhale automatically induces relaxation. Efficient breathing releases tension and pain from the body.

After collectively teaching more than ten million people to breathe energy as well as air, breathing teachers have observed that tetany is a natural symptom of inhibited breathing which clears up naturally when people learn to breathe energy and overcome their fear of body sensations caused by being more alive and relaxed. Relaxed, intuitive breathing is the cure for hyperventilation and all its symptoms.

A rebirthing session may be defined as a person maintaining a connected breathing rhythm for one to three hours in the presence of a rebirther until a natural energy cycle is completed. During this session a tingling or vibrating sensation will begin after five to ten minutes of continued breathing rhythm and continue for one to two hours. This vibrating sensation usually gets stronger and stronger until the body is immersed in it and it climaxes in the middle of a session. After this turning point the energy or tingling sensation recedes naturally, and the person being rebirthed feels deep abiding waves of serenity and a feeling of inner physical cleanliness that is beyond description. This is the completion of a natural energy cycle. The energy flowing during this rebirthing session frees the body from tensions that were held since birth, or tension we absorb from a day of work. If one has never before known what it is like to experience the mind and body without the familiar tensions and inhibitions caused by birth trauma and emotional energy pollution, releasing this trauma creates a state of being that cannot be known through any other means.

The simple breathing practice of connecting the inhale to the exhale for one hour per day seems to dissolve the effects of all kinds of psychological causes, though the accumulation of trauma and tension since birth gives some people difficulty mastering this simple breathing lesson. Most people need five to twenty two-hour lessons to clear the gross accumulated trauma and tension out of their minds and bodies before they can maintain this simple breathing rhythm for one hour without dramatic physical and emotional changes. Rebirthing breathwork can be mastered by many people in ten two-hour sessions with a well-trained rebirther. (I recommend that you interview two or three rebirthers before choosing one to do your ten sessions with.) Going through what is called the hyperventilation syndrome in one or two sessions is a natural part of the rebirthing process. Rebirthing has cleared up hyperventilation, "kundalini casualties," and many kinds of respiratory difficulties.

The phenomenon of the hyperventilation syndrome alarms the medical profession, but it is sanctioned in religious movements under a variety of names. Christians call it the baptism of fire, the filling of the Holy Spirit, or the vibrations of spiritual healing. Eastern religions call it kriya yoga, prana yoga, kundalini yoga, elixir of immortality, spiritual breathing, or shakti, etc. The truth is that regardless of how dramatic or disturbing the hyperventilation experience is, the person going through it is reaching a high spiritual state of physical and emotional cleanliness. With regular practice of the breathing rhythm over a long period, rebirthing produces less and less eventful sessions. Daily practice maintains a wonderful state of spiritual purification with an accompanying sense of mental and physical cleanliness.

Twenty connected breaths can be practiced whenever you feel like it, especially when you are uptight or angry or experiencing other physical or emotional drama.

The breath is the source of the body. Simple breathing along with upgrading the quality of your thoughts about your body can heal everything. The truth is there are no illnesses, only healings. What is called sickness is only a healing in progress. All illnesses and accidents are either the spirit and body attempting to heal the mind, or the spirit and mind attempting to heal the body. We are all physicians who must heal ourselves.

Alternate Nostril Breathing

Following is another profound and simple breathing exercise for spiritual and physical purification. The inhale is pulled softly through the left nostril, held as long as it feels good, and expelled softly through the right nostril. Then the inhale is taken softly through the right nostril, held as long as it feels right, and exhaled through the left nostril. This exercise can be done once, three, or nine times daily. I personally experience that three times a day creates powerful cleansing experiences.

The breath can be held at the top of the inhale as long as it is comfortable, or you can connect the inhale as in Twenty Connected Breaths. You should experiment. In the beginning, you will probably have to use your fingers to close the alternate nostril.

The nose is not just one organ but a whole complex of

organs that regulate body temperature and many body functions. When you lie on your left side, your breathing has a tendency to dominate in and out through the upper or right nostril, and vice versa, influencing different organs.

Fire

Fire is magical and mystical.
Fire is a physical quality of God.
Fire is the warmth and love of God.
Fire is an eternal vehicle of divine grace.

FIRE! So SIMPLE, so amazing! It is one of the ultimate good things in the universe, the source of so many benefits, yet so neglected and unappreciated by people. In fact, most of us are just unconscious of the important and sacred qualities of fire.

Science and technology could not exist without the practical power of fire. In laboratories, factories, and almost all workplaces fire supplies the power. It powers the gasoline engine that does so much of our work today. And yet, the scientists and workers have missed the spiritual power of fire for their own personal health and aliveness. It is no accident that the same science that created ecological destruction with the ignorant use of fire threatens to destroy it all with the ignorant use of fire in nuclear bombs and other weapons of destruction. Obviously, science has been run by mortals. What would happen if scientists became immortal? What would technology and life be like then?

You need to make fire a part of your daily life, because the knowledge of fire can heal your mind and body. A conscious relationship to fire makes us more aware of the miracle of one's physical body, one's mind, one's emotional body, and the Eternal Spirit, which is the source of the fire.

Fire can transform matter into nothing. It can also transform the emotional mind into nothing, yielding peace. Fire is a great spiritual power.

I have met immortal yogis who can sit in a fire without harm to their body or their clothes, even though the flames engulf them.

Fire is our friend; we must use it consciously. It is the highest and most powerful element of the universe, demanding the most intelligence and spiritual awareness to use. Fire purification and fire prevention go hand in hand, so be careful with fire. Fire can burn down your home or a beautiful forest, which might be more fire purification than you'd like!

The basic principle of fire as spiritual purification is to be within five feet or so of the flames, so that the wheels of the energy body can turn through the flames. You want your aura to receive maximum exposure to the flames. After a few days of spiritual purification, my energy body feels clean and balanced again. I feel peace and enthusiasm.

In relation to the purification of the human energy body and healing of the physical body and emotional mind, each fuel produces a different result. My conclusion is that wood is the best. Properly seasoned hardwood is best when sleeping in front of a fireplace or wood-burning stove. It keeps burning all night. However, burning dry brush or small sticks that really make the flames dance high is very efficient at cleaning the energy body. Gas stoves, burning oils, and candles are other fuels; many people in the world burn cow dung. I have a regular routine at home of burning my paper trash. I find that this fire, too, burns away my pain, sometimes in only a few minutes.

Throughout the thousands of years of Bible history, fire was the center of the worship of the Almighty God. The central act of worship for the Hebrews was the sacrifice of animals to the fire, from Adam and Eve to AD 70, when the great temple at Jerusalem was destroyed by the Romans. Actually, the fire ceremony was used in India millions of years before Adam and Eve.

Fire is the power principle of the universe. Fire builds mountains through volcanoes. Fire is the Sun. Fire digests our food. It is the light of day and of the eyes. When humans master the secret of fire, they can do anything.

Fire in the human consciousness is the experience of joy, ecstasy, and creativity. Fire has energy to give us; it is prana, life force. Fire is as important to human health and happiness as food. Sitting with the fire always replaces my tension and misery with joy, peace, and creativity.

You can only and forever learn the secrets of fire from the fire itself. No matter how much I talk about fire, an infinite supply of words cannot reveal these secrets. All true spiritual secrets cannot be revealed by words. And when you know them, no words are necessary.

Fire is a physical quality of God. When I am with the fire I am communing with God. Fire is an eternal vehicle of God's grace. It was used by people millions of years before Bible history and will be used until the end of the Earth and throughout all eternity.

Women and children don't need fire purification as much as men. Women, because of menstruation, have a divine gift from God for a special kind of spiritual purification. The blood is the unity of fire, earth, air, water, mind, and love. Menstruation automatically heals women of more debilities than the rational mind can notice or appreciate. Women are the source of new life and health and aliveness in more ways than just giving birth.

Fire is a daily spiritual discipline for me. I have a simple, personal, conscious, and common-sense relationship to fire. Fire for me is not primarily a physical experience. Fire is a gift of God; it is a spiritual experience. If you value personal immortality, it is not possible without a conscious relationship to fire.

I learned during 1981 when I maintained my own personal fire for a year in the mountains of California that fire has consciousness. Fire is divine intelligence. When I fed it with only very few logs twice per day, I noticed that it regulated its own burning rate so that it never went out. I also observed that it knew how to form a crust on the upper ashes to protect itself from rain.

When I first discovered fire, I wanted to share it with everyone. I wanted everyone to experience the spiritual power of fire and know its ability to heal and restore joy and immortality to humans. I used to always hold our staff meetings around a big fire in the forest.

At a certain point I had to stop this practice for myself. I realized that fire opens the chakras as it releases people's pain, and I somehow feel that pain because the fire makes me very sensitive. I feel another's pain instead of mine, when the reason I am with a fire is to get rid of my own pain. Therefore, I like to be alone. It took me several years to get this sensitive, so if it doesn't bother you to be with groups around the fire, don't worry about it.

The *yagna* ceremony is an exception. There is something about the mantra power and intention of the official Sanskrit fire ceremony that is unique. A yagna is a special fire ceremony led by a Sanskrit priest that offers rice, butter (ghee), honey, sugar, flowers, fruit, etc., to the flames of a fire large enough to consume it. The mantras recited during this ceremony take about an hour. A yagna changes the energy of everyone who participates.

Fire and Community

In every village, town, and city, the fire department should maintain a fire temple or sacred fire. A community fire releases happiness and fosters physical and mental health. Pure fire raises peace and intelligence. If every Christian church were enlightened enough to maintain a twenty-four-hour fire, Christianity might actually work. Let's build fire purification into our civilization. It automatically prevents crime and violence and creates a beautiful atmosphere of spiritual peace in a community.

If fire purification becomes popular, will it cause more accidental forest fires or less? It is a complex question.... Every fire releases prana energy that accelerates the health and growth of trees and plants. Its powerful life energy released into the atmosphere heals and nourishes nature. The ashes make an excellent fertilizer. Each safe fire creates a beautiful spiritual vibration. But one bad fire can cause a lot of destruction. However, even the destruction of accidental fires can heal mass death urge in a community.

The basic elements of a *dhuni* or fire temple include a fire pit in the center and a roof to keep sun, rain, or snow from creating discomfort for the people sitting with the open fire. A dhuni is a fundamental feature in the life of all immortal yogis. Public dhunis could be used by busy people for healing and rejuvenation. An abundance of dhunis in the West could transform our civilization. We should have fire temples instead of bars on every corner.

The Fire Ceremony

When I went to India to seek out the immortal yogis, I watched Babaji do the fire ceremony every day. It consisted of offering rice permeated with melted butter, fruits, nuts, flowers, and sometimes yogurt, honey, or sugar to the fire while thinking or speaking Sanskrit mantras.

It was a beautiful ceremony and it got me up early in the mornings because it was performed at 5 AM. But I didn't get the meaning or point of it. I couldn't feel anything.

The truth was that I was still too dead to feel it. I had been a meat-eater my whole life, and I could not feel spiritual energies very finely. If I could feel the energy of the Spirit, I would have already given up meat-eating. I had believed in physical immortality already for about fifteen years. I had unraveled my death urge a decade earlier. I had been teaching energy breathing to thousands of people for three years. But I was still eating meat, and dead animals in the body deaden our spiritual sensitivities. As a result of being with Babaji for thirty days, I decided to become a vegetarian, which took me a while. This is another story....

In 1981 I became totally enlightened about the spirit and power of fire. After this, I could feel the true value of the fire ceremony.

You may not be as dense as I. You may be ready for the fire ceremony right now. The ceremony is very simple. You build a fire, then offer your favorite foods to the fire. If you like, you can say, "Om Namaha Shivaiya Swaha." It means "I offer to God." Fire is thought of as the Mouth of God. The fire ceremony is an act of love and devotion. The fire ceremony can be done in its simplest form by sprinkling sugar in the flame of a candle. The full *yagna* ceremony is very elaborate. It is probably the most powerful spiritual ceremony in the world. It may be the greatest ritual. This ceremony must be done by a properly trained Sanskrit priest.

Whenever I do the fire ceremony now, I instantly feel an energy rush. My aura is filled with white light and my sensory awareness expands. My vision widens and my eyes see further and more clearly. Negative emotional energy in my body dissolves. However, just sitting with the fire lightens my emotional energy. The longer I am with the fire, the lighter my body feels.

The Name of God

THE KNOWLEDGE OF GOD is the most valuable knowledge on Earth. As Solomon said in Proverbs, "The fear of the Lord is the beginning of wisdom." The practice of the Name is the easiest and most rapid way to spread the knowledge of God. Each year we do the practice, we grow in spiritual wisdom and strength. Practicing the Name is basic to understanding the immortals. The Bible says, "The Name of the Lord is a strong tower; the righteous run into it and are safe" (Psalms).

I studied the Bible and went to church for twenty years, but I never knew what this verse meant until I went to India in 1977. There the practice of the Name is called "mantra yoga" or "japa yoga."

The continuous remembrance of God's Name is practicing the Presence of God. The Name lifts us into God's presence and brings God into our mind and body. For millions of years people in India have been immersed in the culture of Om Kara—the practice of the Name. *Om Kara* means God's Presence or God's Grace and Energy. In India, the form of this practice is to use a string of 108 beads called a *mala* as an aid to concentration and to repeat the Name of God once for each bead.

If you call on the Name of God, don't be surprised if he shows up! Bhartriji and Jesus, Goraknath, the Angels of God in heaven, and all the immortals of heaven and Earth make house calls when you are ready—maybe even before you are ready!

We have 50,000 thoughts per day. How many of them include God? (Crass curses containing God's Name don't count.) Once the practice of the Name is mastered, God is in all our thoughts.

Each Name of God embodies a power. When we master this Name, we master this power. Some Names lead us to historical incarnations of the Father.

In my understanding there is one Supreme Name. It is common to the major religions, although the true pronunciation has been lost to most Jews and Christians. It is OM NAMAHA SHIVAI or SHIVAIYA. "Shivai" is feminine; "Shivaiya" is masculine. The former stands for Infinite Spirit, the latter for Infinite Intelligence. When Thought impregnates Spirit, it gives birth to the Universe. "Namaha" stands for Infinite Manifestation.

"Om" or "Aum" has been changed to "Omen" in Judaism and to "Amen" in Christianity. Some Moslems use this Name also: *"Om Allah ho ya Om."* The Name reveals that all these major religions have their roots in the same God. If you study Exodus, Chapters 3 through 6, you will discover some fascinating detail about the Eternal Name of God. Babaji appeared to Moses in the burning bush and gave him the Eternal Name. This name is OM NAMAHA SHIVAIYA. You can still find it in Hebrew as Ya Vah or Ya Weh. Hebrew is spelled in reverse order from English and its written form has no vowels; thus "Ya Vah" is the last two syllables of Shivaiya in reverse order. The King James version of the Bible translates it as Jehovah. In Hebrew today it is relatively common to say, "Ya Vah Shim Omen."

The religion of the Bible is the same as the religion of Shiva, the Sanskrit word for God. Sanskrit is the spiritual language of humanity. It precedes the Tower of Babel. It is the language of immortal yogis, because there are so many concepts of physical immortality and transfiguration in Sanskrit that other languages have no vocabulary for yet.

Let's make transfiguration legal in the West!

So far in this discussion we are operating at the level of the rational mind, which is subject to eternal argument, as organized religions reveal to us all too abundantly. To create war over God's Name is very superficial religion. When this happens religion is dead.

You can only know the truth of this matter through inner realization and practice.

My practical experience with the Names of God is that they give strength. Earth, air, water, and fire clean and purify, but the Name builds spiritual strength and wisdom.

Further Suggestions
for Spiritual Purification

he Basic Spiritual Purification Program
Step 1: The mind.
Write out on paper or record on tape all your thoughts for fifteen minutes, uncensored. Then go through what you have recorded and change all the negative thoughts into positive ones. Do it again. And again and again until you feel good. One whole day per week should be devoted to this process until you feel good or high all week. Then you can reduce to only one hour per week. You can accelerate this process by doing it every day. This exercise should be done every time you feel low and depressed. It shaves off the bottom of each discouragement. It should also be done during spaciness or hypertense times to discover the source of these feelings. This exercise will eventually yield total peace and control of your mind, your body, and your life. Also for your mind, expose yourself to good literature.

Step 2: Your breath.
Do twenty connected breaths each day—connecting the inhale to the exhale in a relaxed rhythm. Be gentle and conscious on the inhale and relaxed on the exhale. Let go of the exhale such

that gravity causes it—no pushing or holding. In addition, do ten to twenty spiritual breathing sessions with a well-trained spiritual breathing teacher or rebirther. This should include warm- and cold-water rebirthing.

Step 3: Food.
Abstain from food for one day each week for a year. It probably should be a weekday. Weekend days are often social and therefore not good to establish a rhythm. Do only one day per week the first year. Then do two days per week the second year; three days per week the third year. I don't recommend accelerating this program because your mind and body like lots of time and experience to integrate these new food habits and rhythms. It is OK to do half-day fasts and to cheat occasionally in order to process guilt and to learn something about the yoga of comfort and pleasure. Liquids are permitted on fast days. I recommend vegetarianism and fruit diets (eating only fruit and nuts for a week or a month) as a regular practice. Macrobiotics is a valuable diet and so is the raw food diet. Being scientific means that we experiment until we get the healing or the result we desire, then we know the truth about what works. This truth sets us free from diseases and gives us victory and mastery.

Step 4: The Name of God
Sing the Name of God daily. You can sing or chant any name for God, but I have received the greatest value from singing OM NAMAHA SHIVAIYA. The purpose of repeating the Name of God every day is that it evokes the divine presence and all divine emotions. It is wonderful to remember the Name of God constantly throughout the day until it becomes an ever-present thought. This may be the simplest and greatest technique of spiritual purification.

Step 5: Physical exercise.
I recommend that you take a walk every day and meditate upon your neighbors for the purpose of loving them. Be conscious of nature. I do my walk after my morning bath and before breakfast.

Step 6: Sleep.
Stay awake all night once each month. Meditate on the emotional changes and body feelings. Meditate on the moon and the sunrise. Use the exercise in Step 1 to process your disturbing thoughts and feelings.

Step 7: Spiritual community.
Participate in a monthly town meeting on your block or in your watershed. The purpose is to realize a spiritual family and friendships, as well as to fulfill the basic responsibilities of citizenship. If your neighbors aren't receptive to this sort of community, you may want to reconsider being where you are. The more people there are who are interested in physical immortality, the easier it is for all of us. In addition, learn as much as possible from the great saints on Earth.

Step 8: Hair.
Shave your head at least once every ten years. I recommend that during one year every decade or so, you shave your head twice per week (Sundays and Wednesdays) for nine months. This cleans your energy body, heals the physical body, and reverses the aging process. It also accelerates the youthing process.

Step 9: Bathing.
Water purification is simple and easy. I have had the practice of meditating while immersed in a warm bathtub for one hour per day for many years. Taking showers daily is effective, but

I recommend total immersion in water at least once per week. Doing connected breathing while entering the water produces special value, but you can easily experience your energy body— the human aura—by meditating or feeling changes as you enter the water. (See *Water and Air Purification*, below.)

Step 10: Fire.

We have taken fire for granted in the twentieth century. We use the power of fire in our cars, our homes; it does most of our work for us and is the source of infinite comfort and pleasure. In India and in Native American cultures, people practice a ceremony of feeding a fire with ordinary food as an act of respect and gratitude for what fire does for us. American Indians also sometimes give food to their water sources as well to feed the gods of nature. These are good practices.

Step 11: Manual labor.

Physical work is holy. I recommend that you regularly use your body to do housework, gardening, carrying out your own trash, etc. Working with or on the earth produces good feelings and spiritual enlightenment. Farming is the holiest occupation on Earth. Bodywork methods, massage, martial arts such as tai chi, and athletic activities also quality as manual labor. Receiving massage and bodywork is a method of spiritual purification.

Step 12: Population control.

Each person must exercise responsibility for his or her reproductive powers to control population growth. As physical immortality becomes more popular, more conscious child-bearing becomes important. Unraveling the trauma of the birth-death cycle rehabilitates our ability to appear and disappear on Earth by choice. Transfiguration is an acceptable alternative to physical death as a method of reducing overpopulation problems on Earth.

Step 13: Money
Winning the money game through intelligent, enjoyable, and loving service is a method of spiritual purification. Your rewards in life, both tangible and intangible, are directly proportional to the quality and quantity of service that you render to your fellow beings on this planet. See Chapter 15 for more on money.

The revelations and freedom that will be inspired in you as a result of practicing these thirteen simple and natural spiritual purification practices have the power to realize heaven on Earth. Your personal perfection has been waiting for you throughout all eternity. These spiritual purification exercises will open you up so you can let it in. They will enable you to release all of your negativity. They are both fun and enlightening.

Water and Air Purification
The following purification is to be done in solitude. Twice a day, repeat the process below.

1. Fill the bathtub with water.
2. Start a connected breathing rhythm, inhaling and exhaling through your nose.
3. Place one foot into the water while breathing.
4. Continue breathing until physical and emotional changes are integrated.
5. Place the other foot into the water and continue breathing until changes are integrated. For example, some people have warm or cold flashes.
6. Sit down in the tub and continue breathing until changes are integrated. (At this point, you may notice that the exhale is full of excretory material.)
7. Continue breathing until the exhale becomes lighter, more balanced, and more free.

8. Lie back in the water up to your neck, continuing to breathe until the exhale becomes totally light and relaxed.

9. Tip your head back and put your crown chakra (top of head) into the water, and continue breathing until you have integrated the energy changes.

10. Put your forehead under the water, with only your nose and mouth out, and continue breathing in this position until you feel totally relaxed and your energy body feels clear, clean, and balanced. Notice where your energy center is.

11. Experiment by putting your feet out of the water while maintaining the connected breathing and notice the differences in the energy body.

12. Reverse the procedure. Take your head out of the water, sit up, stand up, step out of the water one foot at a time, and keep your breathing connected.

13. Repeat this entire procedure three times.

14. Notice if your jaw is relaxed, your shoulders, legs, pelvis, etc. Give yourself plenty of time! There is nothing like a clean and balanced energy body.

Notes

- Getting completely out of the water and back in three times processes a lot of psychological feelings from your past—mainly infancy feelings.

- Infancy feelings are usually more significant and solid than birth trauma. They are feelings of helplessness and hopelessness in your physical body. Each time you do these exercises you will dissolve some of these feelings.

- Always breathe through your nose at least 90% of the time, not only during conscious breathing sessions but 24 hours a day.

- Most breathing should be done by expanding your upper chest, not primarily with the diaphragm.

- When you do breathe in your belly (diaphragm), imagine a string tied to your belly pulling up. Not only does your belly expand, but the expansion should be felt in your chest, legs, feet, and head. Your whole energy body expands like a balloon on the inhale and contracts on the exhale. Your exhale should not be controlled.

- When you breathe through your nose, the energy that moves in your body cleans the nervous system as well as the circulatory system. Breathing through your nose is much more efficient than breathing through your mouth.

- When your energy body is immersed in water, the energy wheels of your aura are being cleaned by the water. When you combine conscious breathing with bathing, it increases the efficiency of both.

- Practicing this purification in warm water produces completely different results than in cold water. Try different temperatures and see what you learn. Warm means anything over 98.6 degrees; cold is anything under that temperature.

- Water purification gives you the opportunity to experience the physical universe directly instead of your thoughts and fears about it.

- The key to water purification breathing is to relax on the exhale. Another key is to take your time on the inhale.

The Mastery of Thought

Mastery has many levels or stages. Spiritual enlightenment begins with the realization that energy becomes what it thinks about! Thought is the director, the ruler of energy. Energy is the ultimate source of thought, but energy follows and obeys thought.

Thought is the smallest particle of the universe. Thought creates atoms. Thought is also the biggest thing in the universe. Thought creates and surrounds galaxies. Thought is not the source of truth, but the chief executive of truth.

It is essential to master your thoughts. Unconscious and negative thoughts accumulate into emotions which can cause the body organs to malfunction. Negative thoughts and emotions cause tension, misery, and pain, which not only kill the body but also destroy our joy of life and therefore our will to live.

Everybody who dies is killed by thoughts. Our thoughts and habits are manifesting our body the way it is right now. When we master a thought, we master a result. It is personal power.

Obviously to be a conscious master takes most people hundreds of years. The traditional practice of physical death and reincarnation is a needless interruption in our learning process.

People demonstrate in ordinary daily life that they can suspend natural body processes, control them, change them, and cause them, in all kinds of miraculous ways. Our present-time creative power can forever enter into the laws and processes of nature and alter them by pure intention. Life becomes most stress-free when we don't have to deal with supernatural energies and are living in harmony with our ordinary divine and human nature.

We misuse our mind even more than our body by disrespect for or total ignorance of the power of thought. Thought is omnipotent, except for the pure Life Energy which empowers thought.

To build a human body directly out of pure energy with thought is the ultimate level of mastery. To do this, we have to master our ability to manifest thoughts into physical form. This is not difficult. Our thoughts have a natural tendency to manifest into form. We only have to control the content of our thinking—all our thoughts, all the time. Jesus called it "watching."

Fire and the Physical Immortality Machine

In the yoga tradition, this practice is called *Panchagni,* the five fires. Four fires are built, one at each corner of a square about three or four meters apart. The yogi sits in the middle of the fires and stares at the sun, which is the fifth fire. A yogi will practice this day after day until he or she can look at the sun all day, from sunrise to sunset, and also stare at the moon all night. The full form of this practice is of course very advanced. Someone brings meals to the yogi, if necessary.

I've done the five fires a few times with a group. We each sit in the center for an hour or more while the others are feeding and tending to the fires. It is a very powerful practice. It cleans the energy body so quickly and thoroughly that we dubbed it the "physical immortality machine."

This is another exception in which I can enjoy fire with other people, because when I commit a whole day I go through a complete energy cycle with the pain of the group members, and we all feel great by the end of the experience.

It's fun to do this all night to celebrate the full moon.

Fire and the Candle Meditation

Candles are a convenient and popular method to use fire in our daily lives. If you don't have a fireplace in your home, candles can help. I suggest you do the candle meditation to discover how many you need.

1. Set up twelve candles.
2. Light one and meditate for a few minutes on what you feel as a result.
3. Light a second candle and continue meditating.
4. Continue lighting each one and meditate until you have lit all twelve.

5. Somewhere between one and twelve you will notice a result. You will notice movement and improvement in your energy body. This is the number of candles you will need to sit with (or sleep with, if you have a safe arrangement) to obtain a meaningful amount of benefit. You then meditate with this number of candles each day.

I often use candles; I need at least four burning. But sometimes the fumes from the burning wax give me a headache. I experimented with oil burning in a glass and metal cups with a floating wick. I like these much better than candles. Some oils smoke too much, so you need to experiment. Olive oil works well.

It is possible to put water in a glass with the oil. The oil floats on top. When the wick burns through the oil, the water on the bottom automatically puts out the fire. This makes using glass quite safe. In addition, you can put colors in the oil and water to make a beautiful light.

Fasting and Diet

To be immortal you have to give up your fear of hunger. You do this by giving up food until you have certain knowledge you can live without it. Don't try it all at once; do it only one day at a time. The yoga of austerities must be combined with the yoga of pleasure and comfort.

The goal of fasting is not hunger or loss of weight. The purpose is to permit the blood to do its job of cleaning the body. Fasting removes emotional as well as physical pollution. It connects body to spirit and includes the body in the conscious life of the spirit. Everyone I've ever known who ate every other day or less was healthier, stronger, and more intelligent and loving than people who eat every day. Try it for one week and see how you feel. Be a scientist. Your body is the ultimate laboratory.

Sometimes fasting or abstinence is indicated in order to know how polluted we have become. If simple fasting gets you in touch with enough hunger to make you realize how far away from the land and nature you are, then it has started your spiritual purification process. If fasting inspires you to plant your own garden, then it should be obvious that missing a few meals has saved your life.

Be forewarned: Fasting cures some people and makes other people sick. It is recommended that you master the connected breathing rhythm by having ten to twenty rebirthing sessions, then maintain the rhythm for an hour per day for at least thirty days, before you attempt extensive fasting. You should certainly try simple fasts and diet suggestions before doing extensive fasts.

Fasting without breath mastery starts a purification process that can cause a person to relive childhood illnesses. This is why I say fasting cures some people and makes others sick. As a general rule, if you are sick and start fasting, it will accelerate the healing process. If you are well and start fasting, it can purify old psychoanalytical illnesses, and although this process can bring on illness, continued fasting will return a greater state of personal health when the cleansing process is complete. However, sometimes continued fasting will bring on one illness after another, out of the subconscious where they are stored, until the mind is totally free of disease. If weakness or serious loss of weight occurs, the fast should be broken and resumed when you feel well again. When fasting one aims not to produce misery but to produce greater capacity for pleasure and mastery of the mind and body.

If fasting makes you mean and irritable, you should stop. The purpose of spiritual purification is truth, simplicity, and love. If fasting doesn't make you more sensitive and kind and loving, then you should back up and do more thinking and learn breath mastery. Thinking, breath mastery, and receiving loving massage, affection, and friendship are the ultimate techniques of spiritual purification.

It's worth repeating that acts of spiritual purification should be taken in small doses. As soon as spiritual purification exercises produce physical weakness, confusion, depression, anger, or other emotional turmoil, you should stop and resume your normal habits until you feel balanced and secure again. Although feeling "normal" may be a state of extreme illness and pollution, it is OK to return to this state as long as it doesn't kill you or somebody else.

The Bible says that Jesus fasted for forty days and forty nights without food or water. All the immortals of the Bible as well as those in the East did the forty-day fast. If such a fast (and all its prerequisites) were required for a Ph.D., medical, or ministerial degree, then the world would have to cope with a lot less baloney. It is a tragedy that people can graduate from college without knowing that thought is creative (literally), without knowing the power of the human breath, and without learning practical things like massage and fasting. Doing one major fast in a lifetime is not too much to ask to make people conscious of spirit, mind, and body. Fasting teaches us how to care for our bodies and what food is all about. Fasting should be taught in schools.

Limiting your diet to one food item or type of item is a fast. I recommend that you do one- to three-day water fasts once a month for one to two years before trying the advanced forty-day fast. A one-day-per-week liquid fast is plenty for the first year. Then you can expand your limits with your fasting experiments. Your physical body and common sense are the best teachers. Never push yourself or your body. Your psychophysical organism must be gently and lovingly trained. As one's physical body becomes more filled with light, nutrition and fasting become intuitive sciences.

Fasting is an art that takes a lot of experience to master.

Fasting brings up suppressed pain and emotions. A completed healing cycle with fasting should be brief in the beginning. I've seen people get a taste of inner freedom and try to heal their whole life at once. It cannot be done. Slowness is holiness. Whenever weakness or pain comes on, it is best to lie down and devote full attention to your breathing.

Mastering food takes ten to twenty years of practice. Trying to do it too rapidly can make you insane and very sick. It can bring to the surface so much pain that you might try to kill yourself to get rid of it all. When you do it right, fasting is amazingly great. It opens up many new worlds of mind and body. Fasting cleans the blood, the cells, the memory. It can heal anything. It is a great adventure of the soul and can produce more psychedelic effects than drugs. Fasting is more fulfilling that TV, more interesting than working on our house. Fasting is fun!

Sleep is involuntary fasting for most people. It keeps us alive. Eating after sleep is called "breakfast"—breaking our fast for the night. People who fast a lot sleep little. They generalize that food is extra work for the body. Food causes the body to take more rest to recuperate from the burden of processing so much food.

Immortal yogis go for years and even centuries without eating. But they took fifty to one hundred years to master food. If it takes this long to master food, when are you going to start? This week or never? Most people kill themselves with food. If you desire to be healthy, happy, and immortal, you must master food. You must start somewhere. Victory over food is a basic path to the ultimate victory.

Try the following simple diets one at a time:
- First master the one-day liquid fast—juice, then water only. Then go to three days. (When you experience being totally normal and full of energy on the middle day, you will be tasting heaven on Earth.)

- Eat every other day instead of every day and see what it teaches you about the meaning of food.
- Eat only fruit every other week for a month or two.
- Have only milk for a week or a month.
- Be a vegetarian for thirty days.

Scores of books have been written about the benefits of vegetarianism and the ill effects of a meat-centered diet. I do not need to elaborate here, though I encourage you to learn as much as possible about this critical subject. Eating meat destroys the digestive and circulatory systems and pollutes cells. Medical science reveals that eating meat sooner or later kills the body. This is elementary.

Furthermore, if the body is the living temple of God as the Bible says it is, then eating animals is even more barbaric than sacrificing animals on a fire to God.

I learned so much about the divine healing ability of the body through cancer. People who survive it should be given a special degree; it may be more valuable than an MD degree.

Vision Quest

Transfiguration and resurrection are common themes in Native American cultures. Many of these cultures have a tradition of vision quest, in which people are introduced not just to philosophy, but to a real experience of resurrection and transfiguration.

In the classical Native American vision quest tradition, a young adult leaves the tribe and walks into nature alone. This person goes without food or water and perhaps sleep until the vision occurs. The vision is not a hallucination, but an actual resurrection or materialization of a wise person. This wise person offers guidance for the quester's life.

Many young people fail their vision quest. And many who

pass don't do it again. But with some it is a way of life. Meeting with these resurrected wise people is something that can be done more than once. I believe that everyone can have a vision quest annually or even monthly or daily. Some children actually live with a higher spiritual family that they can see, touch, and talk with just like their physical family. It is possible for adults also.

We must resurrect this ability.

Spiritual purification (or austerities) has always been the chief method to reach God. And to bring God to Earth. Sometimes the Eternal Father materializes a body himself. In the American Indian tradition it is usually a Native American spiritual master. The term American "Indian" is considered to be a mistake on the part of Columbus, but I don't think so. Native American cultures and religions are typically Indian, based on earth, air, water, fire, and chanting.

The vision quest is similar to the East Indian tradition of sending young people to caves for meditation. There is one tradition of putting spiritual students in a cave for eleven months, totally dependent upon their guru for food. During this time they are taught telepathically; there is no verbal communication.

The vision quest is a temporary taste of saddhu lifestyle. It raises self-esteem. It teaches respect for nature and appreciation of civilization. It infinitely improves mental and physical health. It makes people strong and more balanced. The vision quest involves all the methods of spiritual purification with mind, earth, air, water, and fire. It is a very holistic and powerful healing method.

I established a gentle vision quest program that is supervised responsibly. The minimum vision quest is one full day and two nights. The participant fasts on water only, bathes twice per day in a hot springs or cold stream, maintains a fire constantly, and is visited once per day by the vision quest supervisor. Ideally it is open-ended, so that the participant can stay longer in the forest if he or she desires. Usually the minimum is enough for the first time. Some people like to do the minimum vision quest annually for a few years. Some participants are in a hurry. They try to achieve total liberation all at once and would likely hurt themselves without a vision quest supervisor.

I've seen people get a taste of spiritual liberation and try to stay out longer than they should and endanger their mental and physical health. You cannot achieve total spiritual liberation in one vision quest. It is not good to push yourself too rapidly. The vision quest is not a compulsive behavior. It must be developed gradually and in an enlightened way.

On the other hand, I've found that God is easy to please. He gives visions without great austerities for most people. Most vision questers have very beautiful and rich experiences.

The vision quest is among the highest kinds of education. I believe that a vision quest program should be implemented in every national forest. It has a totally positive environmental impact. It puts the very best kind of human consciousness in the forest. It cleans the forest floor and prevents forest fires. It creates people who fall in love with the forest and become protectors of it. It cures the ills of civilization. It heals people. There should be volunteer wardens of every forest—divine stewards.

Every forest should have a fire temple that is available to people for fire purification. Fire temples are good for human ecology as well as our natural resources. If we had fire temples also in city parks, it would be possible to do a vision quest in the city. People who live in the city can easily go to the mountains or desert on a weekend and quickly rejuvenate themselves. It is an ideal practice for professionals to prevent or cure burnout. When done regularly, it can dissolve the stresses of successful living and renew creativity and energy.

There is a Sioux tradition of doing an annual fire ceremony for three days with fasting, singing, and dancing. These kinds of traditions can accelerate the realization of physical immortality. The Hopi Nation is the spiritual capital of the North American continent. I try to do an annual pilgrimage to Hopiland. My personal practice is to sleep on the land for three nights. I usually experience a total renewal during these three days in Hopiland, even if I sleep in the Cultural Center Motel and watch TV. The energy of Hopiland is so pervasive that nothing can keep you from getting the benefit.

The basics of immortal yoga exist in Native American cultures. Even conventional scholars admit that the Hopi Nation and culture have been stable for at least 80,000 years. Will the United States Nation last this long? Will even the Christian religion last this long? Ram, Sita, and Hanuman are still popular after 100,000 years. Will Jesus Christ and Moses be this popular after 100,000 years?

Spirituality and Your Automobile

When you are driving, try to remember that automobiles are meditation machines. They require a high degree of intelligence and courage. Never before in history have people faced the opportunity to come inches away from death many times per day as they do routinely when driving down the highway.

Automobiles are one of God's favorite vehicles of spiritual purification for the present generation. Cars often trap people alone and force them to meditate. If the drivers don't think deeply enough to solve their emotional problems while driving, their cars break down or have accidents. The fact is, there are no accidents, only emotional problems looking for a place to happen.

Automobiles allow people with a highly developed death urge to kill themselves without creating wars. Private ownership of automobiles and public commercial airlines has probably done more to prevent World War III than all the orthodox Christian churches and expensive modern universities put together.

Personal Mastery and Citizenship

U NLESS YOU FEEL GOOD about living as a hermit in a cave, being an immortal yogi master requires plenty of attention to your community. Responsible citizenship is an essential element of the practice of love.

Politics is a golden opportunity for adult education and spiritual enlightenment. Community is an opportunity to nourish our neighbors and be nourished by them.

The American tradition of town meetings provides a vehicle for the expression of community. It takes a practical master to actualize this opportunity, because everyone is waiting for someone else to initiate the action in most communities. Neighborhood representation is another powerful idea. I share it with you in brief form below. If you would like to pursue it, you can write to me for more information at P.O. Box 118, Walton, NY 13856.

The fact is, democracy is disappearing—in the USA and around the world. Everyone has the feeling that government is not serving them, and no one is willing to do anything about it.

Democracy is the rule of the people: Government controlled by the governed. Government of the people, by the people, and for the people. *Republican* means that the people rule themselves through elected representatives. Republican democracy is dead today because the people—the voters and citizens—no longer care about their elected representatives. In fact, if you do a survey, you will discover that almost no one even knows who their elected representatives are.

The problem didn't occur overnight or even in a year. It started more than two hundred years ago after the U.S. Constitution was written. Population expansion gradually eroded the principle of representation until today our representatives don't care who we are. And we don't care who gets elected. Voting in elections is a meaningless act for most citizens; many don't even vote at all.

The only way this problem can be solved is by electing a neighborhood leader for every thousand people who becomes a full-time professional government watcher for the citizens. This elected neighborhood representative can inform us about what our other representatives are doing and can begin to reshape local, state, and national (even international?) governments so that they again become the servant of the people instead of our masters. Our elected neighborhood leader is our only hope of regaining control of government.

There is no other way. We cannot have government of the people, by the people, and for the people without the people. Without neighborhood representatives and a monthly town meeting we are powerless.

There is either participatory democracy or no democracy. But how do you get the "people" to care and to participate? This question leads us to psychology and spiritual enlightenment. Why are the people apathetic, ignorant victims?

The only way the "people" can be enlightened, inspired, and educated is to have a neighborhood leader on every block who can spoon-feed them information when they need it or are ready for it. So how do we get a leader-teacher in every neighborhood elected and paid?

It has to start with you and me. I am willing to be one, so you can vote for me and contribute $10 or more per month to my support. Ten dollars doesn't seem like much, but if I can get a thousand people to join you with the same monthly contribution, it becomes $10,000 per month. With this monthly budget I now have the time and resources to influence our elected representatives for your benefit and mine. If current elected officials don't respond, we will have the grassroots political power to replace them. If you are also willing to be an elected neighborhood leader at large, I will support you and work with you until you succeed.

The Psychology of Politics and Apathy

Most people are programmed by their parents to do nothing without permission. And they are taught to get approval before trying something new. Therefore, as long as existing elected representatives are waiting for the voters to give them approval, and the voters are waiting for approval from their elected government officials, change can never occur.

People are afraid of new ideas, because they are afraid new ideas will garner disapproval from others, or even punishment. Politics is handicapped by psychological problems, and apathy is caused by the parental disapproval syndrome. Almost every child was unjustly punished by parents at some time. The child reacts by deciding not to cooperate, by not participating in the parents' approved activities and projects. The rebellion syndrome develops. The child disapproves of the parents to get even.

Most adults today act out this immature emotional syndrome by not being responsible citizens and by not participating in their community. They also are stuck in the money syndrome—not having any time or energy after earning enough money to survive.

As a result of the layers of complicated bureaucracy that

have evolved to replace citizen participation, apathy has almost totally killed the spirit and reality of republican democracy in the U.S. and elsewhere.

Bureaucrats by definition can't do anything without permission. The idea of serving the people has been lost. Humanitarian motivation is considered to be quaint, obsolete idealism.

Our income tax system is total corruption. Citizens have become unconscious slaves of the IRS and Federal Reserve system, which is a private corporation. I won't go into it here, but I'm pointing out to you that your lack of political responsibility costs you money—one to three days' worth of income each week. When are you going to wake up and stop selling yourself to ignorance?

The knowledge of your natural divinity will cause in you a tendency to exercise your divine right and authority to reconstruct republican democracy so that it serves you. But people have layers of emotional trauma that must be healed before they can become rational and responsible citizens. Who will heal them?

Obviously only an enlightened leader on every block is sufficient to do the job, but where are these enlightened leaders going to come from? How will they be trained? Who will elect them? How can citizens who don't care elect anyone?

Is it possible to find one intelligent person out of every thousand citizens who cares enough to get elected? If we do find a person who is willing, what problems will be encountered in the process of healing the citizens enough to get rational and responsible participation?

Obviously the process itself is the training program. But who will get the process started? Who is spiritually enlightened? I have waited in vain for thirty years since I wrote my first book on the idea of neighborhood representation for someone else to do it. Where is the intelligent and sensitive citizenry? Where are responsible people? Spiritually enlightened people? Finding one is like a spring in the middle of the desert.

One of the practices that can resurrect republican democracy and create heaven on Earth is the town meeting. Such a meeting heals people on all levels: spiritually, politically, emotionally, economically, socially—it can even heal physical diseases. But getting people to participate can be hard work. The town meeting has to be offered to people weekly or monthly for a year or two. It takes long-term continuity to cure habitual apathy and unconsciousness.

The weekly town meetings can be supplemented by seminars that fully explain the concept of elected neighborhood representatives and how the system works within existing political structures. The seminar will explain spiritual enlightenment and freedom of thought, speech, and religion. Everyone needs a basic education in citizenship and responsibility.

Financial Aspects of Citizenship

I would be remiss in this book about physical immortality if I didn't share with you the idea of government without taxes. You have heard it said, "Nothing is certain in life but death and taxes." It is amazing to me to talk with people and discover how willing they are to be imprisoned by death and taxes and be proud of it. Victims love bondage and punishment. The Bible says that the punishment of sin is death. I can only conclude that people spend more time thinking of themselves as sinners rather than dwelling on their natural divinity as the offspring of God.

Jesus said, "The sons of a nation don't have to pay taxes." I don't know the exact history of this statement, but if you really understand money, taxes are truly unnecessary. The following statement (condensed version) took me thirty years to write. I've read it to thousands of people, and everyone says, "Yes! This is the way it is supposed to be." Then they do nothing about it.

Money doesn't have to be complicated. Following are the secrets to money, both personal riches and public finance. You will be able to pay the national debt just by copying and sharing these ideas.

First and foremost, money is a means of exchange. Exchanging what? Wealth. Wealth is ideas, goods, and services. Money is not wealth, but a means of exchanging and measuring wealth. Money is ones, zeros, and paper (now computer chips).

Money is also a merry-go-round. All the money you don't have, other people have. You and I get our money by supplying other people with goods, ideas, and services. We can easily double our income by serving more people. Personal creativity applied to the loves and goals of other people is the source of loving service that leads to riches. You can have fun winning the money game by supplying your own loves and pleasures in life to others who share your tastes.

Now for a revolutionary lesson in macroeconomics that will really get you excited! Money is a means by which buyers and sellers (also called consumers and producers of wealth) exchange their ideas, goods, and services. In simple terms, economies are composed of laborers and consumers, who are obviously the same people trading with each other.

This means that the proper source of money is the buyers and sellers, the citizens, us! We are the natural source of the money system. We have the natural right to create any kind of a money system that serves us in exchanging our wealth. Money is the servant of the people, not the master.

In other words, we have the natural right to print money. We also have the legal right to print money. Yes, we do! We do not have the right to print Federal Reserve Notes—this is forgery—but we do have the legal right to print money. We exercise this right every time we order personal checks at a bank. Every time we use a credit card, we are printing money out of nothing at our local store. You and your local merchant are printing new money to assist you in the transition of exchanging ideas, goods, and services.

Understanding money and the money system is big business, and now I'm going to show you how to cash in on it.

As a citizen of your country you can own the money system. Money is a social experience of communication and agreement. The value of money is determined by the buyer and seller in every transaction. All transactions are negotiable and optional. Everything can be purchased without money if you have enough creativity and salesmanship or something to trade. Profit is the creation of new money out of nothing but the imagination of the individual business person. It is put in the bank when someone pays the profit.

Taxes mean we produce to earn money to give to the government to buy what we produce—it is double work. We can just authorize the government to print the money for our community project needs. It should certainly be possible to have government without taxes. The government, like a giant dinosaur, is eating our farmers, our businesspeople, etc. Government taxes suppress the poor, private enterprise, the arts, support for the environment—the list goes on and on. Fortunately we learned in school that we own the government. So why are we doing this to ourselves? Ignorance. We are ignorant about money and about our citizenship. But no longer! You are now becoming enlightened and armed with the truth. The Federal Reserve Bank is a private corporation, and the very rich people who own it are collecting the interest on the national debt. Your ignorance is worth billions of dollars every year to them. How long will you stay ignorant? How long will you be a slave of the IRS? If you pay income taxes to the IRS, you are an ignorant slave.

If you claim your natural and legal power now, you can instantly increase your income as soon as you eliminate taxes. As the source of money with the power to print money, we the people can end taxes altogether. We the people can authorize our government to put a credit in its checking account for its annual budget. When we use our natural right as citizens to create a money system that serves us, taxes are unnecessary. We can authorize our government to print money, then we must supply the ideas, goods, and services which we authorize the government to buy. The government can only buy from the people what we produce.

Remember, the U.S. Constitution gets its power and authority from us—We the People!

I have given only a brief overview of these ideas here. (You can write me for more detail.) They may seem tangential to the subject of physical immortality but I think not. Taking control of public and private finances helps lift us out of ignorance and free us from the death-inducing effects of constantly struggling for money. It is also basic to enlightened citizenship responsibilities.

Conclusion:
So You Are Immortal—What's Next?

AFTER WE BECOME IMMORTAL, there is nothing to do but become beautifully human. Babaji is a beautiful human being. Jesus was a humanist. He didn't even excommunicate Judas. To be divine means to be a humanitarian.

To be fully human means to take normal care of the body, to have wholesome mental and spiritual disciplines such as mantra yoga, bathing, conscious breathing, proper diet, exercise, sleep patterns, a relationship to fire, and a satisfying career. To be divinely human means to relax and be at peace with the world, to enjoy the sun and moon and seasons—to live as ecologically as possible.

To be human means to live with people in kindness and patience. A conscious human participates appropriately in community and politics.

To be a divine human being means to accept each stage of life and to enjoy it: childhood, teenage life, young adulthood, family life, career, senility, etc. It means to gather the wisdom of human existence. We can be victorious, without fighting what is natural. We can learn to heal ourselves.

We don't have to live the second century before we complete the first. The natural human condition is filled with beauty and goodness. Life and the world are good! They are the gifts of God for our pleasure and learning.

To be a divine human being means to live truth, simplicity, and love—to treat people with kindness.

It means to resist evil. Babaji said, "To practice nonviolence does not mean to stand by and watch injustice while doing nothing." It means to get involved. It is not kindness to watch one person hurt another. To practice nonviolence means to prevent violence. Prevention takes creativity and action.

Humans are given 50 to 100 years by God and nature to heal ourselves emotionally and to realize our natural divinity. If we liberate ourselves from birth trauma (includes womb and infancy consciousness), parental conditioning, the misuse of thought, the unconscious death urge, trauma from previous lives, senility, and education and religion trauma, then we naturally become immortal.

If we master spiritual purification with mind, air, fire, water, earth, and loving relationships with people and God, then we are immortal. If we do a good job with our first hundred years and are beautiful, natural human beings, then what? We will get another hundred years.

What will we do with them?

Why wait to be human after we are immortal? Why not become a beautiful human being now? Why not view the human experience as the supreme path of enlightenment? Planet Earth is a perfect school! Just be!

Maybe it doesn't take a lot of intelligence to pay for a home with indoor plumbing, warm water, electricity, and a fireplace. With a little meditation and pranayama, diet control, fire, and soaking in a warm bath, anyone can become immortal.

We don't have to throw away our civilization; we only need to correct it a little. We can reduce population expansion. We have the technology for pollution-free automobiles. Electric cars are a reality—why aren't you using one?

A little asceticism is also richly human. Babaji participates in the world for 25 to 50 years, then he leaves the world for 25 to 50 years to enjoy just living the love of God in nature. We can taste asceticism in small doses until we love God more than the world. Practicing the Presence of God is the ultimate state!

It may take us 50 to 100 years just to be able to love and to be free of hate. To be a rich human being means to love people and to love God and to enjoy being loved. Most of us are damaged by centuries of spiritual and emotional corruption—perhaps hundreds or even thousands of lifetimes' worth of soul pollution. It will take us as long as it takes to heal. But the sooner we start, the easier and more pleasurable life becomes. We no longer have to live misery. Spiritual enlightenment and spiritual purification are the answers.

Physical immortality is not difficult. In fact, it is the most pleasurable way to live. Being an immortal yogi master is no more difficult than supporting a family for 25 to 50 years and putting one's children through college. It takes the same kind of focus. To be immortal, we only have to focus on the extremely pleasurable (if ordinary) habits of personal aliveness and to avoid the habits of death. Unfortunately, the habits of death (eating meat, for example) are programmed into us by our parents and approved of by orthodox religion and the public schools.

The alternative to living in the death dream is to endorse your own natural divinity and to be intelligently responsible for your own health and healing. When we become responsible for creating our own death, we can also choose to be responsible for creating our own life—developing the habits of personal aliveness and health.

The biggest barrier to both physical immortality and transfiguration is always the same—ignorance. Basically it is ignorance of one's self. This includes philosophical ignorance, emotional ignorance, ignorance of the body, and ignorance of nature. The three biggest killers are ignorance, emotional energy pollution, and poor diet.

Profound openness to God, to feelings, to the body, and to nature can produce eternal life. It is a practical eternal life that includes our physical body and can include our family and friends.

Living with the idea of physical immortality is the richest kind of living. It is living fully extended, with joy and peace and wisdom. Living with our eyes open to the Light of Life is different from living in darkness and ignorance with no knowledge of God, no understanding of the meaning of life and the body. It is mortal existence or immortal existence. We can live in harmony with eternity or in fear of it.

The secret to aliveness, of course, is the love for God. Practice the Presence of God and be a humanitarian who maintains sufficient spiritual practices with earth, air, water, fire, and love. In one sentence, this seems to be the gospel of everlasting life and personal aliveness.

Physical death may not be the path to heaven and to God, as is popularly believed in most religions. It may be running away from the light. Physical death may be an excuse and escape from true godliness.

However, the immortals teach and illustrate that physical immortality is not the primary goal of human life. The goal is truth, simplicity, and love. Physical immortality and transfiguration are only ordinary parts of the supreme goal. They illustrate the Truth.

Abundant life is a balance—balancing earth, air, water, fire, and mind. Balancing creation and destruction. Balancing accumulation and distribution. Balancing intellect and experience. Balancing purification and pollution. Balancing expansion and contraction. Balancing permanence and change. Balancing action and inaction. Balancing energy and stillness.

The person who masters balance masters body, mind, and spirit and gets to live forever in wisdom, love, and grace.

Love is the willingness to process the negative energy of other people. Even if it is possible to participate in the world without getting dirty, I don't know if it is desirable.

This book is by no means perfect or complete. I've shared some introductory and (I hope) valuable concepts about physical immortality. About four thousand years ago Moses said, "I've set before you the ways of life and the ways of death; therefore choose life that you may enjoy your days upon the Earth" (Book of Exodus). We know what they chose.

Mastering physical immortality is not that hard. We only have to move away from those thoughts and habits that are known to produce death (like cigarettes, eating meat, and participating in orthodox religion) and to embody those thoughts and practices that are known to enrich our personal aliveness (like meditation, seeking peace and wisdom, conscious breathing, bathing, eating right and fasting, fire purification, productive work, and loving relationships). Being a normal, relaxed, productive human being who practices the Presence of God is not that difficult.

The source of the kind of evil thoughts that lead to death is not tuning into God every day. If we allow greed, hate, and unconsciousness to keep us running in a life of tension and imbalance, we have a natural tendency to forget God and lose our bodies.

On the other hand, achieving physical immortality is as complicated as the complexities of our own soul. We have to harness our own mind. We have to unravel all the emotional patterns we absorbed from our parents. We have to heal the trauma of previous lifetimes. And we have to choose enough worthwhile goals to keep us interested in material existence on planet Earth. God knows, there is enough to do! Some people think they are better than God if they lose interest in the eternal drama he has created to keep us as well as himself interested.

It is important to think of ourselves as immortal human beings and to build this thought into our self-image. Yet thinking we are immortal is irrelevant until we are at least 300. Until we have mastered 300 years of human life, it is unrealistic to claim to be immortal. In fact, it is still unrealistic until we have an invulnerable body of light that we are the total master of.

I experience year after year that doing the simple spiritual practices with the elements systematically makes the human mind and body healthier and lighter all the time. My experience is that the practices produce not only spiritual success, but worldly success as well.

Babaji once said, "I could heal you all in one day, but then what would you learn?"

The process of life is also the goal. The purpose of life is to teach us wisdom—the wisdom and value of energy, thought, and physical reality in existence. Wisdom is both spiritual self-sufficiency and interdependence. Simplicity sometimes means to surrender to the complexity of life. The supreme wisdom may be the realization that we are all God stuff playing in the human drama.

Look, seek, and understand inside and outside. It is all here! Lift yourself out of desperation and PLAY! The immortals are always playing in our drama. When will you begin playing with them on the stage of the cosmos?

The choice to be an immortal yogi master makes you immortal in the present time. The trick is to stay immortal. This obviously involves mastering this choice in the Eternal Now. We are right now the masters of this instant; we only need to extend this mastery to the next instant, and the next, remembering to be the master of our lives.

To receive a list of available books, tapes, and videotapes on physical immortality, rebirthing, and related subjects, contact the author:

Leonard Orr
Inspiration University
P.O. Box 118
Walton, NY 13856

Telephone: (607) 865-8254
Fax: (607) 865-8247